Depression, Stress, and Anxiety

A Guide to Master Your Emotions

Olivia Bauman

conjunction with this work. The Publisher acknowledges that the reader acts of their own accord and releases the author and Publisher of any responsibility for the observance of tips, advice, counsel, strategies and techniques that may be offered in this volume.

Table of Contents

Table of Contents

Introduction

Do you want to know how to come out of the clutches of depression, stress, and anxiety?

Do you occasionally experience uncontrollable negative emotions that seem to ruin your entire day? Do you feel that you are not good enough for anything in life? Well, guess what? This is something that many of us experience, so you must first stop feeling alone. We are in this together. Sometimes all you need is a little assistance to deal with the day-to-day stress that accumulates in your life, often leading to anxiety and depression, and that is exactly what we will be doing here – this book will act as a guide to help you find your way.

That being said, understanding your own emotions and acknowledging them is the first step, and this book will help you with that too. Once you have identified your emotions and specifically pointed out the ones that are causing the problem, you can use the strategies to reprogram your emotions to see the world in a different way. Just keep in mind that no matter how damaged or broken you may feel, there is always hope and a happier life is possible for everyone!

In this book, you will learn why people develop depression, stress, or anxiety, the underlying causes of these problems, and what steps can be taken to step out from their clutches. But in the end, I would also like to remind you that these things don't develop overnight, and in most cases, they take months or even years of trauma or bad experiences to develop such situations; hence you should not expect them to go away in a day. You have to be patient and continue with the strategies mentioned in the book, and after a certain point, you will definitely notice changes.

There are plenty of books on this subject on the market; thanks again for choosing this one! Every effort was made to ensure that this book is full of as much useful information as possible, please enjoy!

Chapter 1: Symptoms of Depression, Stress, and Anxiety and Their Underlying Causes

Are you feeling under the weather? Is your head feeling heavy? Are you under a lot of stress? In our daily life, we experience many stressors. From academic stress and household duties to stress related to office work, 'stress' has become a constant in our lives. However, while you can't avoid stress, you also can't let it build up. Accumulation of too much stress can lead to anxiety and mood swings. And slowly, you may fall into the clutches of depression, which is something you don't want to experience.

Stress, anxiety, and depression do not come knocking at your door suddenly overnight. These things gradually develop over time. And one leads to the other, and the entire chain forms a vicious cycle that is extremely difficult to break without proper treatment. These three form the root causes of various other physical and mental illnesses that can slowly eat away at your life. They are like a slow poison, gradually killing you from within.

As I mentioned before, to live a healthy and prosperous life, you can't afford to have too much stress in your life. It affects your performance and decreases your efficiency over time. It is the root cause of severe mental illnesses and requires long treatment. To battle stress, we need to know how it is caused, where it arrives from, and what its symptoms are. Let's look at all of these in more detail.

What Is Stress? Is It Good or Bad?

In medical terms, stress is nothing but a feeling of heightened physical or emotional tension. It can be caused due to any event or thought which makes you feel worried or nervous. Stress is the normal reaction generated by the body in the form of intellectual, emotional, or physical responses when changes occur. It is the body's response to upcoming challenges (stressors) or demands. So, is stress good or bad for your health?

Stress can be either positive or negative. Positive stress, also known as *eustress* or good stress, is the feeling that you get when you are excited about something. According to many psychologists, having positive stress in life is beneficial and can help boost your performance and work rate. Positive stress isn't harmful, so it should neither be avoided nor a cause of concern. In fact, it helps you stay alert, motivated, and ready to take on any challenge that may come your way. But, what must be avoided is high amounts of negative stress. Stress becomes a problem when the stressors continue for long periods without a break of relaxation in between. This is when it turns into negative stress. And, you need to prevent this negative stress from accumulating inside of you.

Causes of Stress

You can experience stress for a number of reasons. This can be due to work pressure, unstable finances, academic pressure, bank loans, relationship cracks, family problems, recurrent health problems, or everyday inconveniences. Depending on your situation, any of these examples can be extremely stressful.

Stress usually triggers the body's *flight-or-fight* response mechanism to counter the impending threat or danger. In this state, your body releases certain hormones like cortisol and adrenaline, which increase your heart rate, enhance blood flow to all your major muscles, slow your digestion, and change various other autonomic nerve functions to give you an extra boost of strength and energy to fight off the challenge. When the perceived threat is over, your body automatically returns back to its normal state, which is called the *relaxation* mechanism. However, in the case of long periods of stress, the relaxation response mechanism does not occur at frequent intervals, and therefore your body is unable to return back to its normal state. The more your body stays in the 'flight-or-fight' survival mode, the more damage your body incurs due to the heightened body metabolism over long periods.

You can feel stressed either because of one big event in your life, or from a build-up of many smaller things over time. Therefore, for the second scenario, you may be unable to identify what exactly is causing your stress or when it actually began. And therefore, you may find it difficult to explain the cause of your stress to other people or even your counselor. Let's look at some of the common scenarios where you can feel stressed and exhausted.

- You are feeling the mounting pressure or heat at your workplace.
- You are tense and worried about something.

- You are facing discrimination and are being subjected to hate and abuse.
- You are unable to control the outcome of a situation or how it unfolds over time.
- You are going through a tough and uncertain time that is challenging your responsibilities daily.

Stress is not in our hands, except in certain scenarios. Some situations which may not bother you at all, might become a big reason for someone else's stress. It is because we are all influenced by various experiences in our lives and have different levels of perseverance and ways of coping. Certain events may become your causes of stress, but they might not be the only ones. Many people often become stressed when things get out of their control, and they have to think too far ahead to determine all the plausible outcomes. Are you facing stress in a similar manner?

Personally, you can feel stress in a lot of ways. You can have stress due to illness or injuries, a failed pregnancy, from suffering harassment and abuse, committing criminal acts, repeated failures in life, or losing someone close, or other related matters. These cases make you stressed at a personal level and can cause problems in your daily life. Even stress due to family matters can fall under this category, such as breaking up with your living partner, losing your children, having a difficult relationship with your parents, siblings, children, or friends, or lack of proper income, or unpaid dues. Losing your job, sitting at home unemployed, or lack of productivity are some other instances where you can experience stress. In all these cases, you need to exercise patience and perseverance to calmly survive the situation and prevent the stress from building up inside of you.

Symptoms of Stress

We all know how closely our body and mind are connected and the overall impacts that one has on the other. In fact, you can better understand the connection if you are currently undergoing stress. The impact of stress is evident not only from the deteriorating mental condition but also from the decline in physical health. Feeling stressed out over lack of finances, failed relationships, or unhealthy living situations can create various physical ailments. Don't think that you can have physical health problems only if you are stressed and not the other way round. The inverse also holds equally true. Health problems, such as high blood pressure or acute diabetes, can affect your stress levels and the state of your mental well-being. Our body reacts accordingly to the amount of stress we're experiencing.

So, how can you realize that you're stressed? Are you over-stressed? When should you be alarmed?

Stress is not easy to recognize. In fact, in many situations, it remains silent and doesn't surface until later. However, if you're careful and observant, you will recognize certain signs that can reveal whether you are stressed or not. These signs show whether you're currently under a lot of pressure. Sometimes, stress can occur from an obvious source that you know from day 1, whereas, at other times, piling up of stress can happen due to various small things such as pressure at school, workplace, family, or friendship, which can leave a heavy toll on your mind.

Whether you're dealing with chronic stress, a stressor that occurs daily, or a major challenge in life like a permanent illness or divorce, the stress in any form can take a significant toll on your body, both mentally and physically. So, how do you know what signs you should look out for if you want to effectively deal with stress? What are the things that will give you a clear indication of whether or not your mind is facing any additional pressure? How can you realize that the level of stress you are undergoing is unhealthy for you?

Let's look at those indications more closely, which can potentially reveal the amount of stress you're facing.

- **Emotional signs** – If you're stressed, you have likely been through similar situations. Stress can make you feel irritated, angry, moody, and easily frustrated over time. Your emotions speak a lot about your present condition. Good emotions reveal a happy mind, whereas negative emotions showcase stress, anxiety, and frustration.

- **Psychological signs** – Do you feel a lack of concentration when you're clearly worried about something else entirely? Well, it is a sign of psychological stress. This form of stress constitutes signs such as difficulty concentrating, greater worries, anxiety, and even forgetting things. Your memories often become clouded if you are reeling under stress and you can't even remember what happened the day before or the day before that.

- **Behavioral signs** – Under acute stress, you can often forget to take proper care of your health and well-being. You experience distress because you can't properly enjoy all the happy moments you're undergoing or rely on drugs and alcohol to numb your pain.

- **Physical signs** – Stress will cause your blood pressure to rise and increase your heart rate. Chronic stress can also reduce your body weight and weaken your immune system; which can cause you to be frequently affected by colds or other gastrointestinal diseases, which weaken your daily metabolism rate. Women can also notice certain changes in their menstrual cycle. Both male and female people may also notice a decline in their libido and sexual capabilities.

If you're experiencing any of the following, you can take it as a sign that you're feeling stressed.

- **Headaches** – If you're very tense about something, you can feel your head being tightly held or wrapped around from the sides. You may also find the tightening feeling to gradually increase over time. Frequent bouts of headaches are a clear indication of acute stress.

- **Sleep Disorder** – Stress affects your normal sleep pattern. As I mentioned earlier, chronic or acute stress does not allow the body to return back to the normal state from the flight-or-fight response mode. Hence, your body is unable to sleep and rest all the senses due to long periods of heightened metabolism. As a result, you may find yourself staying awake the whole night. If it continues for days, your body will become completely exhausted and weak.

- **General Anxiety** – We, humans, are usually anxious creatures. But, if you're feeling anxious for long periods, it is usually due to the presence of many stressors in your life. An increase in anxiety can be directly linked to heightened stress.
- **Frequent Colds** – Besides diseases, stress can also be a major factor in lowering your immunity. When you have greater amounts of stress, your effective immunity decreases, and so does your body's ability to fight off foreign invaders. If you're under too much stress, you become susceptible to every ailment and may fall sick more frequently than before.
- **Frustration** – Having multiple causes of stress can be quite demanding. You are bound to get frustrated after a certain point, which would lead to irritation and anger. This adds to the difficulty in relationships and stands as an obstacle to your personal happiness.
- **Confused Memory** – Under severe stress, your mind may not be able to think properly. You can get easily confused, and even the easy details may seem lengthy and painful. The flight-or-fight response mechanism is designed for tackling short periods of danger and not for sustained periods of stress. When triggered in excess, this stress response can actually delay your thinking and your ability to find a quick solution.

These are just some of the many ways by which stress can affect our bodies and minds. Don't forget to consult a doctor if you're feeling extremely stressed or having frequent bouts of it.

What Is Anxiety?

Often you have heard of the term anxiety, but do you know what it is? What does anxiety actually mean? And, when is it caused? What are the symptoms that can tell whether a person is feeling anxious or not? You might not know the answer to all these questions, do you? Well, let's look at anxiety in more detail, along with its causes and indicators.

Anxiety, as you may know, is your body's response to an impending event. It is different from excitement. Anxiety is usually associated with fear and worry rather than happiness and delight as in excitement. Anxiety often causes cognitive issues like difficulty in breathing, tenseness in muscles, shaking of fingers, difficulty in concentration, and others. It may only be a normal response of your body, but in certain cases, it can grow into a chronic disorder.

How Is Anxiety Caused?

Anxiety is nothing but anticipation of a future threat. As humans, we all feel anxious at certain points in our lives. Be it your school exams or your company project submission, or before a risky operation, we have all experienced anxiousness. However, not all of us undergo an anxiety disorder. It's normal to be anxious about the important events in your life, like your first job interview, a drama performance on stage at your school, childbirth, a first date, or any other important occasion. But, when you start worrying too much, and it gets out of control, to such an extent that you start worrying for every big or small occasion, your anxiety develops into an anxiety disorder.

Anxiety disorders are characterized by excessive fear, hypertension, and other related behavioral and physical changes which can worsen over time. These conditions manifest as both mental and physical symptoms and can impact your daily life and relationships. Anxiety disorders come in many forms, like generalized anxiety, social anxiety and others, and should not be confused with day-to-day worrying.

How to Know If You Are Suffering From Anxiety?

Like other ailments, anxiety has its own symptoms and indicators that can clearly tell how anxious you are or whether you are suffering from extreme panic. People diagnosed with anxiety disorders like panic disorder, often experience various uncomfortable physical symptoms. These include accelerated heartbeat, shaking of hands and legs, trembling, and profuse sweating, among the major ailments. Because of the severity of these symptoms, people suffering from panic disorders or increased anxiety require immediate medical attention. Ignoring these signs can prove to be dangerous or even deadly.

If you are suffering from hyper-anxiety, you might feel that your anxiety symptoms are actually controlling your life. You can be afraid of an impending panic attack, avoid people due to social anxiety, or just be constantly worrying for no actual reason. Sometimes, it can get you agitated and irritated for absolutely no reason at all. To get yourself treated, you need to first understand the symptoms, so you can recognize which type of anxiety you are currently facing and what type of treatment you require. Not all anxiety disorders are the same, nor do they involve the same treatment.

Anxiety gives rise to a combination of various psychological, social, and physical symptoms. The exact characteristics of the symptoms differ from person to person as it is based on the type of anxiety the person is facing, the individual circumstances that the person has gone through, and other personal triggers. Let's look at some of the symptoms of the various anxiety disorders.

Generalized Anxiety Disorder

People who are suffering from this type of anxiety experience excessive fear, worry, and anxiety that are very persistent and hard to control. Some of the major symptoms of generalized anxiety disorder are:

- Fatigue
- Difficulty in concentration
- Irritation and restlessness
- Muscle tension and soreness
- Lack of sleep

A person is said to suffer from GAD if he/she shows most of these symptoms, along with worry or anxiety, for a period of six months. For children, only one of the above symptoms, along with anxiety or worry is sufficient to be diagnosed with GAD.

Social Anxiety Disorder

Earlier known as social phobia, social anxiety disorder is characterized by excessive fear of social and on-stage situations. If you are suffering from this type of anxiety issue, then you may start behaving inappropriately due to extreme anxiety when you are supposed to meet new people, speak in front of others, do any public activity, or even maintain your relationships. Social anxiety disorder has the following symptoms:

- Excessive anxiety and fear in public places
- Sweating profusely
- Rapid heart rate
- Upset stomach or nausea
- Avoiding social contact and intense fear of social gatherings
- Overly self-conscious and self-judgmental
- Social and occupational impairment

Children who have this type of anxiety exhibit symptoms such as throwing tantrums, refusing to speak, crying and clinging to the body in the presence of other children.

Panic Disorder

It is a mental health condition where you experience unexpected and repetitive panic attacks. Do you know what a panic attack is? A panic attack is a moment of extreme fear and physical discomfort that almost feels like a heart attack. Let's look at the symptoms of panic attacks.

- Shortness of breath
- Rapid heart rate and heart palpitations
- Feeling choked
- Chest pain
- Feeling near-death conditions
- Profuse sweating
- Trembling and chills

People having a panic disorder experience repeated outbursts of panic attacks and develop extreme anxiety about such situations in the future. They tend to avoid any situation that can give them a panic attack.

Post-Traumatic Stress Disorder

You probably have heard about PTSD, right? Anyone who has fought in wars knows very well what PTSD is. It is a type of anxiety that develops in people as a response to the extreme trauma they witnessed while fighting on the battlefield, suffering irreparable lifelong injuries, facing near-death moments or being subjected to sexual violence. However, not only soldiers or police personnel but anyone can have PTSD, which includes symptoms like:

- Social detachment
- Lack of sleep
- Difficulty in remembering the details of the traumatic event
- Exaggerated response
- Lack of positive emotions such as satisfaction and happiness
- Self-destructive behaviors
- Recurring flashbacks and psychological distress from involuntary memories
- A negative outlook on themselves or the world
- Persistent negative emotions such as guilt, fear, and horror.
- Avoiding triggers related to the traumatic event
- Irritability and hypervigilance

What Is Depression?

Okay, so now you know what stress is and how it is caused. You also know about its symptoms and how it can affect people like you and me alike. You also read about anxiety, right? And after reading about its various types and symptoms, you can perhaps make an idea of how serious they are in your mind. Well, both stress and anxiety are vicious. And, in fact, they both cause each other and are therefore sort of interrelated. Similarly, they both also lead to depression when they are persistent for a long time.

Depression can be defined in medical terms as a period of persistent sadness, very low mood, and diminished interest in whatever is happening around or the activities which previously seemed enjoyable. Depression occurs due to a combination of various social and psychological factors like trauma, stress, anxiety, illness, and family history. Depression has long-term symptoms that can leave a major impact on a person's life.

If you're facing depression, you might face difficulty in performing your daily activities. Sometimes, you may even feel that your life is no longer worth living. Depression isn't just a bout of blues or a normal weakness; it's something from which you can't just snap out of. It requires long-term treatment, and even after that, there is no guarantee that you will never feel depressed again in life. But don't get discouraged.

Causes of Depression

So what causes depression? Is it the same as anxiety and stress? Or are they different?

The answer to what exactly causes depression has not yet been clearly defined. But it is believed that it happens due to the result of several factors, including genetics and the person's personal situation.

From the continuous research conducted by medical practitioners, they have discovered a new cause of depression. Medical researchers now believe that depression can be an inherited condition. It is believed that certain genetic changes make the neurotransmitters that regulate our mood ineffectively or scarce. Research has found that in almost 40% of cases, genetics has been able to successfully determine depression.

Another key factor that can cause depression is the practical situation of the person. Certain cases may occur to a person more likely than the rest, such as:

- A family history of fighting bouts of depression, either among the parents or among the siblings.
- Financial troubles due to unpaid debts and tight finances.
- Experiencing a major change in life, such as the death of a family member, loss of job, serious illness, or divorce.
- Undergoing chronic ailments that cannot be cured.
- Resorting to illegal drugs and alcohol or overdosing on prescribed medications to relieve pain and suffering.
- Taking medications that can cause depression as a side effect.
- Lack of proper nutrition in their diet.

- The person is undergoing immense stress, which releases the hormone 'cortisol' affects the neurotransmitter serotonin, and leads to depression.

If you have previously experienced depression, you may experience it again at a later stage in your life.

Symptoms of Depression

So how can you recognize when you are feeling depressed? Are these signs enough to tell us that we are depressed? Well, people experience depression in different ways. Some people may only exhibit a few symptoms, whereas others may exhibit multiple such symptoms. In fact, some symptoms can get better with time, whereas others may deteriorate over time and get worse.

To understand why you are depressed and how to deal with it, you need to know which depression symptoms you are currently exhibiting. Only then can you determine the best approach to deal with them. Clinical depression can be of various types, and each has its own list of symptoms that help to classify which type the person belongs to.

Major Depression

It is also known as unipolar depression or major depressive disorder. Don't get confused. This is the depression that mostly comes to mind when you hear the word 'depression.' Let's look at the symptoms to better understand them.

- Loss of happiness and enjoyment from daily life
- Lack of interest in hobbies and work
- Feelings of emptiness and sadness
- Lack of adequate sleep
- Tiredness, fatigue, and exhaustion
- Loss of appetite and weight
- Feelings of worthlessness and guilt
- Fixation on past failures and self-blame
- Inability to make decisions
- Extremely agitated or silenced
- Planning about death or attempting suicide
- Angry outbursts due to frustration, even over small matters
- Anxiety, agitation, or restlessness

Bipolar Disorder

Depression can also lead to another mental health condition known as bipolar disorder. Do you know what that is? Well, if you suffer from bipolar disorder, you actually switch back and forth between severe depression and heightened mood known as 'mania.' You tend to exhibit two types of emotions at the same time, both in extremes. The depressed phase of bipolar disorder has symptoms similar to major depression. However, in the greatly elevated phase or the manic phase, you can exhibit completely opposite symptoms such as:

- Increased energy
- Racing thoughts and rapid speech
- Irritation
- Increased libido
- Poor judgment
- Lack of sleep and impulsivity

Teenage Depression

Did you know that there was once a thought that children and teens could not have depression? They thought that children simply could not feel depressed at such an early age. However, now we all know that that is entirely false, and kids and adults alike can face depression in their lives.

School-going children show symptoms of depression such as loss of interest in school activities, lack of interest in going to school, not hanging out with friends, scoring poor grades in exams or any other similar scenario. Similar to teens and adults, children suffering from depression also experience a lack of sleep, loss of appetite and body weight, hair loss and physical pain like headaches and stomach pain. Children suffering from depression should be immediately treated to avoid serious and unpleasant situations.

Worry is part of our everyday human lives. But, if you think you are worrying too much compared to the importance of the situation, you may have developed stress. Maybe it's time for you to go and consult a doctor or a counselor. Stress, if built up for too long, can give rise to serious anxiety issues and ultimately lead to depression. You should never imprison your feelings and issues, as it will only make matters worse.

Anxiety symptoms can only worsen over time if left unnoticed. In fact, many anxiety conditions go undiagnosed and untreated. If you let your fears roam freely in your mind, you will start to avoid situations that you previously cherished. You may find yourself totally isolated from the outside world, locked up in your room and distant from even your friends. Sustained levels of anxiety and stress develop into depression and may drive you towards drugs and alcohol abuse.

Serious bouts of anxiety can make people afraid of going out in public, returning phone calls or even meeting with their friends. You can also develop various physical ailments within your body that can only deteriorate over time unless their root cause is treated. And, in the worst case, you will get affected by depression.

To effectively deal with all these ailments, you need to keep a positive mindset. You can't allow the negative emotions to settle in and take over your mood and behavior. Exercise is often considered the best remedy to fight off bouts of anxiety, stress, and depression. Along with exercise, socializing with your friends and relatives is also important to fight off isolation.

And, if all these do not seem effective in fighting off these ailments, hurry and consult a doctor for treatment.

Chapter 2: Practice Self-Compassion

Have you ever thought about how to treat yourself properly and why it might be important? Most of us are too quick to beat ourselves up over the slightest mistakes. We as a society are perhaps to be blamed for this because from a young age, we are taught to evolve through self-criticism. But what we thought would bring us success, may have had a boomerang effect on us; we take self-criticism to an extreme where it cripples our confidence and it may result in affecting our mental health greatly.

Pause for a moment and think about how you treated yourself the last time you could not meet a goal or made a mistake that perhaps led to your failure. Did you beat yourself up when things went wrong? Do you think you were harsh on yourself? It probably led to a sense of dejection, and you kept telling yourself that you were no good. Such negative self-talk can stress yourself out, make you anxious, or aggravate your anxiety and depression. Well, the truth is that you are not the only one, most people tend to be hard on themselves, and including them, you too can be a little more compassionate towards yourself.

Several studies on the subject have concluded that self-criticism sabotages our wellbeing and results in negative outcomes. These studies have further revealed that self-criticism lowers an individual's self-esteem and it may also lead to anxiety and depression.

Self-compassion, therefore, is pivotal to both psychological and physical well-being. Forgiving yourself and nurturing your emotions will not only ensure good health but will also improve your relationships and bring about a positive change in your overall well-being. There are several benefits of practicing self-compassion and one of the most important benefits is that it has been proven to reduce levels of anxiety and depression in individuals. Those who are self-compassionate will inevitably realize when they are suffering, and being kind to themselves at such times can reduce a lot of their suffering. It takes away a lot of their worries and anxiety, as well as depression that may be related to it.

While many people are already self-compassionate and the quality may come to them naturally, many are yet to learn. The good news, however, is that self-compassion though is inborn for some; it can be learned, practiced and mastered by anyone at any stage in their lives. Let us look into some ways to help us cultivate self-compassion and how it may ease our anxiety, depression, and stress.

Self-Compassion - Myths and Facts

Compassion, as we know, is the ability to show concern, empathy, and love for people who are in some kind of difficulty and self-compassion is the ability to show the same kind of love, acceptance, and to be understanding towards one's own self. Self-compassion for some may sometimes feel like self-indulgence, but it is neither selfish nor self-pity. Kristen Neff, an associate professor at the University of Texas and also a self-compassion researcher, was the first to define the term. According to Kristen, the term self-compassion has three key elements –

1. **Self-kindness** – This means refraining from being harsh to one's own self.

2. **Recognizing the humanity that one possesses** – This means realizing that you are not the only one struggling, no one is perfect and everyone experiences pain. When we struggle, we tend to feel lonely and isolated. We may think we are the only ones who are making mistakes, failing, or experiencing loss. But in reality, these struggles are part of our shared experience as humans.

3. **Mindfulness** – It means maintaining an unbiased experience of events and observing life without being judgmental or suppressing your own feelings.

The lack of self-compassion can prove to be harmful to one's self. People who go through a troubling or traumatic experience find it difficult to feel self-compassion as they view it as self-pity. For instance, many emerge out of a divorce feeling guilty and shameful. They may think that their marriage has failed and, as an extension, begin to see themselves as a failure. They may feel undeserving of a second chance or a chance to heal from their troubles. Such judgments towards themselves may hinder their growth and give rise to insecurities.

Going by the results of research conducted, self-compassion can be effective in helping one recover from post-traumatic stress. Apart from depression and anxiety, therapists too highly recommend practicing self-compassion.

Self-compassion may be a new practice or skill for many of you, and there are chances that you may get caught by myths that exist around it. Before you proceed to make it a practice, you must be aware of the myths that exist around it and get your facts clear. Following are some of the myths that Neff has dispelled.

- **Self-compassion is self-pitying** – Self-compassion is about being aware of your situation, acknowledging your hardships, and seeing things just as they are. While you acknowledge your suffering, you also acknowledge that others may have similar problems and therefore, it is not ego-centric at all, contrary to what many think.
- **Self-criticism is a motivator** – Neff says that there can be nothing motivating about criticizing yourself; all it does is make you lose confidence and faith in yourself. Criticism is an old method that cannot bring results anymore; self-compassion can be effective in helping one grow. The habit of self-compassion acts as a supportive and nurturing parent.
- **Self-compassion is being self-indulgent** – Being self-compassionate is not the same as seeking pleasure. It is alleviating suffering and not being slothful. It is putting your problems into perspective and assessing what could hurt you in the future.

Strategies for Self-Compassion

We can pretend to the external world, but we cannot fool ourselves about the way we feel, just like an athlete who keeps playing with a cut under their foot. If the athlete wants to continue with the game, they too have to stop, assess their wound, treat it and then continue. This is what self-compassion is. It is acknowledging what the situation is and addressing it accordingly. Otherwise, the athlete will be in more pain and will find themselves more stressed. The same is the case for any individual who is facing any emotional trouble. To take care of your needs, you will need to acknowledge them first, and that will be possible if you show yourself compassion.

There are several ways in which you can apply self-compassion when you are feeling anxious. Following are a few suggestions that you can start with.

- **Practice forgiveness** – You will need to be in acceptance of your flaws and realize that you are not perfect; therefore, you are bound to make mistakes. Stop penalizing yourself for every mistake you make. Be gentle with your shortcomings, and keep reminding yourself that those who love you, value you not because you are flawless but because you, are you. At times when you start deriving your self-worth from the precision and perfection of your actions, you must become aware and remind yourself that you deserve love however you are.
- **Be grateful** – The feeling of gratitude is essential in the practice of self-compassion. When you appreciate the things you have, rather than focus on what you lack, your

attention automatically shifts from your shortcomings, and your inner voice gets gentle.

- **Have a growth mindset** – If you view challenges as obstacles, then you are bound to stress out. Instead of avoiding challenges, embrace them and find meaning in them. Instead of feeling defeated or threatened, seek inspiration from those whose success makes you feel insecure or makes you question your abilities.

- **Write a kind letter to yourself** – Have you ever written a positive message to a friend who is undergoing a stressful time in their life? This is the same exercise, the only difference being that you will have to address this message to yourself in the form of a letter or a note. You may have never done this before, but it does work well. You can start by writing about the things you are good at or the traits that you appreciate in yourself. Encourage yourself with some love and kindness just as you would to someone having a hard time.

  Another approach to this exercise could be maintaining a journal where every single day, you pen down the things that you are proud of having done on that day. Journaling can have other benefits like – it can help you explore more about yourself. It can help you to know who you are, what things you like about yourself, your feelings, and where and how you would like to put your energy.

- **Pen down the self-criticisms** – The negative self-talk you have in your mind, write all of that down on paper. It can be anything like 'you are so dumb,' 'you are worthless,' or 'you will never make it.' Write down all the things that you have been criticizing yourself for. We do not usually say such things to people we love and we try to be supportive and understanding, but when it comes to ourselves, we become our worst critics. Putting down the criticisms on paper can help you to look at your remarks objectively and show you that perhaps you are not deserving of such harsh words.

- **Think about how you would treat others** – When practicing self-compassion, the best way to do so is to look at your situation objectively. Imagine that someone you care about has come to you after failing at something or getting rejected. Take a moment and think about how you would treat them. Would you say something like 'you deserved it, or 'you are good for nothing'? Treat yourself like you would treat your loved ones.

- **Watch what you say** – Criticizing ourselves is a habit for many and sometimes we get so used to it, that we do not even notice when we sabotage ourselves. Therefore, paying attention to the words you use for yourself can help you identify if you are being self-critical. Now consider if you would say that to your dearest friend. If not, then you are being self-critical.

- **Use physical gestures to comfort yourself** – Experts say that kind gestures can have a calming and soothing effect on our bodies, activating the parasympathetic system. Neff says that physical gestures can help break the negative narrative playing in our heads and get us back to our bodies. It is in our nature to create our own storylines, and our minds run away with the narratives we create. Physical gestures like placing your hand over your heart or holding onto your arms tightly can be enough to comfort us and bring us back to reality.

- **Use positive affirmations** – Repeating positive affirmations regularly can be helpful in getting back your confidence and handling your anxiety. Some examples of positive affirmations are-
    - I am doing very well and I will keep getting better.
    - I am a kind and loving person.
    - I will see obstacles as learning opportunities and will overcome them strongly.
    - I have the capability to change the way I feel about this situation.
    - I am worthy of love and kindness. My worth comes from who I am and not from external circumstances.
- **Use compassionate phrases often** – Whenever you catch yourself saying something discouraging to yourself like 'I am horrible,' stop and reconsider what you are saying. You may instead tell yourself that 'I am going through a tough time, and this suffering is a part of my life. It is not my whole existence and

does not define who I am. I need to show myself some love and compassion to alleviate my suffering and deal with this.' Such positive affirmations, when paired with physical gestures like putting your hand over your heart, can be powerful. It can make one feel calm and diminish their anxious thoughts.

- **Try using releasing statements** – The words that you say to yourself when you notice that you are speaking unkindly to yourself are what is meant by releasing statements. They are a great way of letting go of unwanted thoughts and embracing your real emotions. Say, for example, you are at a social gathering, but you are feeling uncomfortable, and your anxiety is kicking in. You tell yourself that you have no hope, for you are terrible at socializing. It will make you unlikeable as a person, and you will never be able to make friends. In such a situation, instead of replaying the harsh criticisms constantly in your head, acknowledge that you are feeling anxious. Tell yourself that it is okay to feel the way you are feeling and that you will overcome it.

  The motive behind using releasing statements in such scenarios is to free your mind from troubling thoughts. It helps you to accept your real feelings and move on. It does not mean that you will be able to stop feeling anxious right from the moment, but this strategy will help you to manage or have control over how much you let your emotions discourage you or make you upset.

- **Take a self-compassion break** – When things get tough and you are being too harsh on yourself, taking a quick break can be a good way to improve the situation. Do something nice for yourself, like making yourself a warm drink like coffee, or indulging in whatever makes you feel better.

- **Comfort your body** – Remember that your body and mind are all interconnected and how you feel reflects on your physical health. Some ways to give your body comfort and take care of yourself are –

    - Eat something healthy.

    - Lie down and take some rest.

    - Give yourself a quick hand, neck, or foot massage.

    - Take a walk in the open and get some fresh air.

  Anything you can do to improve the way you feel will be your dose of self-compassion, and it eventually will get you to sail through your hardships without taking a toll on your overall health.

- **Practice mindfulness** – Mindfulness is said to have a positive impact on self-compassion. Try to be in the moment and be aware of what is happening around you in the present, without trying to judge or label it. Allow yourself to feel what you want to at that moment; neither do you have to curb your emotions nor announce them to everyone.

Allow your feelings to come and go without getting attached to them. Practicing mindfulness meditation can be beneficial.

Meditation is an excellent way to retrain your brain. Practicing guided meditation and loving self-kindness meditation are ways to make the self-soothing and self-compassionate gestures more soothing. The most effective and essential way, however, is to have a self-care routine and to take good care of your body along with your mind. When your personal wellness declines, you are likely to direct negative feelings towards yourself, which can also affect your ability to show compassion towards others. You can follow the strategies mentioned above and easily cultivate self-compassion. It is quite a patient practice and takes some time to master, but it can bring about positive results in reducing anxiety and boosting overall health.

Chapter 3: Maintain Emotional Hygiene

Say you tripped and got a wound on your knee. You would definitely tend to the wound, right? You would clean it, apply antiseptic and cover it up to prevent it from getting infected. But what would you do with a wound that is psychological? Do you not think that you should treat it with the same care, so that your emotional trauma may heal too?

What Is Emotional Hygiene?

It is known to all of us that a human body has two components – the mind and the body, and they work together as a single unit, and taking care of both of them is essential to living a healthy life. From early on in our childhood, we are encouraged to practice hygiene in order to prevent illnesses and to help us to look after and take good care of our bodies. But did you know that it is important to look after your emotional or mental hygiene too? To maintain personal hygiene, we brush daily, eat healthily, and ensure our bodies are clean as well as our surroundings. But how does one keep their mind healthy and clean? Before we get on the ways of doing so, let us first understand what emotional hygiene is since not all of us are familiar with the term emotional hygiene or are well aware of it. Guy Winch from Psychology Today observes that "Emotional hygiene is being mindful of our psychological health and adopting brief, daily habits to monitor and address psychological wounds when we sustain them." The psychological wounds can be of many kinds and range anywhere from losing a person you love, to failing at something. Sometimes rejection and chronic loneliness can also be reasons for psychological injuries. They have a harmful effect on both our minds and bodies. Depression and anxiety are the most common mental health troubles that arise out of psychological injury, while a rise in blood pressure, increase in cholesterol levels, and hindrance in the proper functioning of the immune system are the physiological problems that may arise.

Noticing these wounds and tending to them is what can be understood as the practice of maintaining emotional hygiene. It refers to being aware or mindful of your stress, suffering, and emotional traumas, monitoring them, and taking the initiative in the form of daily habits to heal from those.

How Can You Practice Emotional Hygiene?

Your emotional hygiene too benefits from your daily practices, like in the case of physical hygiene. They, too, require putting in the daily effort, focus, energy and time. The following is a guide to help you with taking care of your emotional hygiene.

- **Pay attention to your emotional pain** – In the case of physical pain, our body generates sensations in order to alert us, and the same goes for emotional pain. If you are unable to overcome a rejection, a failure, or a bad mood for days, you have sustained a psychological wound that requires treatment.

  In order to conquer your emotional troubles and heal from your pain, you need to be aware of what is bothering you or hurting you. Be attentive to your emotional pain and act on it whenever you feel that you are suffering, do not push it away or be passive about it. If you feel low emotionally, take a break, talk it out with your friends and family, or a therapist if you need to.

- **Stop disregarding your emotions and give yourself time to heal** – We often have the habit of dismissing our issues, thinking that they are not worth the attention, and keep pushing them away. Address the issue at hand immediately without thinking that it is small. It is likely for you to feel that the reason behind our pain does not have much significance, but if at any moment you feel that you are getting upset over it, you should not disregard it. We do not heal in one day; it is a lengthy and time-consuming process, but remember that a day will come when you will have healed, no matter how big or small you think the issue is.

- **Keep negative thoughts away and try to avoid setting out on a guilt trip** – The fact that you are hurting is not your fault. If you often have thoughts like, you are good for nothing, or you do not deserve good things to happen to you, then you need to keep away from such thoughts. One of the most important aspects of emotional hygiene is self-esteem which is necessary for our survival. Learn to show yourself some compassion and make yourself believe that you are worthy of doing and receiving good things.

Just as guilt is harmful to your emotional health, so are depressing and negative thoughts. They unnecessarily clutter your mind, taking away your attention from the process of healing. When you find yourself in such a situation where negative self-talk and bad thoughts are clouding over your mind, engage in a distraction. Do anything that would take your attention away from the noise in your head. You may solve a puzzle, go for a walk, paint something, or whatever will keep your mind off of defeatist thoughts.

- **Reconsider the way you respond to emotional trauma** – You may not be able to change the event, but the outcome is in your control which you may change. For instance, you have failed at something. The situation is irreversible; it has been done. The way most of us respond to a situation like this is to sulk, beat ourselves up for our shortcomings, and end up sabotaging the little confidence we have left. Such a response benefits you in no way and only creates a negative effect on your mind. Failure can make you focus on what you cannot do instead of what you can do. The cycle of focusing on shortcomings keeps continuing if not checked.

  The other way of responding to the event is to acknowledge the situation and learn from it. Instead of crying your eyes out and stressing yourself, you can write down all the things you did correctly in the process and the things you could have done better or differently. Assess your mistakes by paying close attention to them and stop blaming yourself for the failure.

Your decisions and actions may have led up to that result, but have faith that you know better and can do better than that.

List the factors that will be in your control the next time you give it a try. Plan and prepare for the areas that you can improve on the next time. Such exercise will help you to feel less helpless and improve your chances of succeeding in the future. The key is to be persistent, and your efforts will surely pay off.

- **Look after emotional bleeding** – When you get a cut, look after it and try to prevent bleeding from the same area. You ought to take care of your emotional bleeding too. Though emotional wounds cannot be seen, they may run deeper than surface cuts and can take time to heal. They have the chance to recur and can create vicious cycles. To stop the bleeding from a psychological wound, you will have to ensure that you do not hurt it by contemplating. You will need to correct the situation by planning, being patient, and by putting in consistent effort.

- **Change the negative self-talk** – Remember, the things you tell yourself are your thoughts and not established facts. Thousands of thoughts come to our minds on a daily basis. Some of them are positive, some neutral, and some negative. To ensure good emotional hygiene, you will learn to have to challenge such pessimistic thoughts and gain a balanced perspective. Whenever you encounter negative thoughts, you can challenge them by asking questions like – "Where is the evidence that proves the truth of this thought?", "In what other ways can I view this situation?" "What words would I use for a loved one who is going through the same situation as me?" This is a matter of practice, much like learning a new skill, but you can always start by being kinder and more compassionate towards yourself.

- **Practice self-compassion** – Negative self-talk makes us doubt our abilities, hurting our self-esteem. Practicing self-compassion is a great way of healing our damaged self-esteem, which you have already read about in the previous chapter.

  You must learn to quickly overcome your emotional drawbacks in life, which requires patience, time, and a good amount of self-love. Being kind towards yourself and showing self-love will help you raise your resilience in turbulent times, making you feel stronger, and then it becomes easier to heal emotionally.

- **Stay informed** – An essential prerequisite for taking care of your emotional hygiene is being aware of yourself and knowing what works for you and what does not. What works for others will not work for you similarly; what works for you will not be effective for others since emotional hygiene is a personal thing. Observe closely what makes you feel good, what ways enable you to heal, and successfully keep you away from the habits that further degrade your mental health. Other than just knowing ways that suit you, you will also need to have access to the resources and information required to heal.

- **Practice self-care** – Look after yourself and do things that will refuel your emotional tank. Self-care means doing all that is essential to keep both your emotional and physical health well. Activities like riding a bicycle, watching the television, and going for a swim can help you unwind and give you a much-needed break from the clamor in your head. Self-care does not always mean being indulgent. It also means being firm yet kind to yourself, such as going to bed at a specific time or eating healthier rather than indulging in your guilty pleasures.

Some other tips that will help you to maintain your mental hygiene are –

- **Have your basic needs covered** – The first step we need to take to feel okay is to satisfy our basic needs like eating and resting well. They are the key to our psychological health, and at no cost should they be allowed to slip.

- **Boost your self-esteem and learn to trust others** – In order to be able to enjoy good mental hygiene, it is essential that we accept the way we are. We must believe and have faith in ourselves. At the same time, we must also learn to be trusting.

- **Learn self-control** – Learning to manage your feelings does not mean disregarding or shutting off your feelings. It is more about having the knowledge of identifying them, interpreting them, and regulating their intensity so that you may be able to respond to them in an appropriate way.

- **Think positive and block negative emotions away** – We often find ourselves plagued with fears and doubts, which can be challenged and blocked by keeping a positive outlook.

- **Try to relax** – Whenever we are faced with adversities, our body reacts naturally to them and gives rise to stress. As you already know, stress may lead to mental health issues like depression and anxiety or may act as fuel for your anxiety.

- **Seek support from loved ones** – Humans are social beings. Like you interact with others to have fun, you can also share your concerns with those you trust.

Remember that having good emotional health does not mean that you are always happy and free from all kinds of negative feelings. It means having the resources and skills to deal with the troubles of daily life. In the present times, anxiety and depression have become the most commonly faced mental health issues especially post the pandemic. But, the worst part of mental health issues is how easily they make their entry into the other aspects of our lives and end up affecting even the most mundane part of our life, like brushing our teeth or taking a shower. Therefore, to live a healthy life, you should prioritize your emotional hygiene in the same way you make maintaining personal hygiene a priority.

Chapter 4: The AWARE Approach for Anxiety

Anxiety is considered a stress reaction. A reaction that can gradually lead to an anxiety attack. It is essential for you to know that you are not alone in this; there are 40 million other American adults affected by this yearly. The purpose of emphasizing the number is simple - to let you know that it is okay to not fight it or focus on trying to hide it from the world instead of on yourself!

If the only person next to you during the time of a panic attack tells you to fight it or that you are overreacting to your fears, do not get demotivated. Or even if it is you who always tries to chase away the attacks, then you need to stop immediately. Trying to suppress the attacks will do you no good, at least not in the long run; it will rather embed negative notions in your head.

Negative notions like running or avoiding problems or stress can be beneficial for a very short-lived period, but they will only affect you adversely in the long run. Your panic attacks will keep coming back if you do not let them pass their course. Now the question is, instead of fighting it or trying to suppress it, what should be done? To answer this very question, in this chapter, I will discuss the AWARE approach that will help you deal with anxiety attacks by yourself.

The AWARE Method in Layman's Term

AWARE is an acronym for a five-step method that can help you find some comfort during anxiety attacks. The acronym stands for –

1. Acceptance and Acknowledgement
2. Wait and thereby watch
3. Anticipate and/ or take Actions
4. Repeat the three steps mentioned right above
5. The End where you expect the better

The acronym is just to help you remember the steps in the right order. This five-step method will help you to cope with anxiety in a way by reducing the fearful and all-consuming thoughts.

You and your loved ones, need to understand and recognize that it is difficult, in fact, perplexing, and can be emotionally and physically draining to cope with anxiety attacks. However, it is possible to find comfort in such situations and the AWARE method will help you achieve that. It is also important to note that this proven method can help you cope with mild anxiety attacks, but if you are someone who gets severe anxiety attacks or faints during one, then you should always consult a counselor besides trying these self-help methods.

In the next section of this chapter, you will learn in detail the five steps that will serve as a guide on what to do and how to handle anxiety attacks while performing a chore or task.

Step 1: Accept Your State, Circumstances, and Situation

The one most important step that paves the path for finding comfort is acknowledgment and acceptance. Accepting that you are scared and anxious is a crucial step that most people tend to overlook. However, the truth is that progress starts right in this very first step of AWARE.

Acknowledge that you are getting anxious, fearful, and perhaps about to have a panic attack. Do not try to fight it or do reckless things to distract yourself at the moment. I know all the readers have different ways to distract themselves during their panic attacks; some tend to tell themselves to stop thinking about the emotions, whereas some are probably snapping rubber bands on their wrists as soon as they feel the obsessive emotions powering in.

However, does all of this work? When you are telling yourself to stop thinking about it repeatedly, all that you are doing is fueling the fire even more! The constant pressure from yourself or anyone telling you to fight it adds more stress on top of what you are already going through and more often, it only worsens the situation.

Instead of all this, just appreciate the present, the reality. It is okay to acknowledge the fact that you are scared; you feel anxious that something might happen. Acknowledge that all these emotions are out of the fear that you are in some danger, but the danger is not real. Remember and keep practicing to realize that the feeling of fret is just another expression of anxiety and is not to be paid much importance.

Overcoming an anxiety attack is possible only once you start working with it and not against it. Imagine you are having a severe stomachache that you dislike; what do you do in such a situation? Do you tell God to take it away, and it goes? Or do you blame yourself for the ache? You wouldn't hit yourself in the stomach, because you know that doing so, will not help the situation.

Similarly, in case of a panic attack, you accept that you are scared. You accept that it will pass, and you cannot possibly over-power it by fighting it. This is the first and foremost step that you must somehow achieve.

Anxiety Attack: How to Accept It?

It is easier to say "accept the situation" than to practice the same in real-time. Thus, in this section, I will help you to learn to accept the situation. Let us start by looking at practical examples to help you understand how you can accept an attack.

In general, there are different types of attacks; some can kill you, some can hurt you and the rest are dreadful but do not kill you. You should know that an anxiety attack, although in no way desirable, is acceptable as it falls under the category that does not kill you. It is a moment when you are extremely overwhelmed, vulnerable, and feel dreaded, but it will eventually pass without killing you.

What might kill you is a robber standing in front of you with a gun in hand. This is an unacceptable circumstance, and you can in no way trust the robber and should hide from him or her and their gun at all costs. You can yell, bribe, beg, run, fight or even hide from them to avoid things from going wrong.

However, when you are speeding a car beyond the limit of the road or breaking a traffic signal, the police ought to give you a ticket. This again is something not desirable but can it be accepted? Yes, you should accept it instead of trying to bribe them, yell at them or run away from them. Trying to defy them will only escalate the situation. Thus, stop trying to resist the symptoms, and that is one of the best ways to accept an attack.

How Can Your Panic Attack Affect You?

Most of you might have multiple questions from the previous section that boil down to this one greater question: what does a panic attack do to me? The answer is simple; it makes you scared and vulnerable. You start dreading something scary happening to you, around you, or to your loved ones. A panic attack affects you by making you imagine the worst happening to you.

To tell you the truth, if you have a panic attack, then you are already there, at the worst. A panic attack is already serving the purpose of scaring you and reacting in a way that upsets both you and your loved ones. Thus, although from the surface level viewpoint, it may seem like the panic attack is just making you anxious as it causes you to imagine and see the worst, the truth is, it is the worst.
The dreadful things you are imagining are imaginary and may or may not happen; the danger causing your feet to sweat is also not real but a mirage. Therefore,

you are already at rock bottom, and what do they say about rock bottoms? "Once you hit the rock bottom, you can only go up." The journey or the path may not be as smooth, but you can eventually swim back to the top by simply accepting it.

Do not resist it. The less resistance from you, the closer you will get to overcome your anxiousness and the attacks. This also explains why you should choose acceptance of the symptoms of panic attacks instead of trying to resist, deny and push back the symptoms.

Always remember, a man who tries to fight the rain and demands sunny weather during the monsoon, suffers terribly. Resisting the weather is in vain. You will suffer less if you just accept that the weather cannot be changed by you and carry an umbrella. There will be discomfort, but you will sail through the day victoriously. The choice is yours –

1. Resist the weather and suffer.
2. Accept the weather and acknowledge that the weather cannot be changed, and carry an umbrella to get things done.

AWARE's first step is to help you learn that all you need is an umbrella to float through the attacks in much less discomfort.

Step 2: Wait, Take a Moment to Observe

Having an anxiety attack means that you are about to or have already entered the fight or flight mode. This gets activated when we are in danger and helps us to quickly and safely escape the peril. However, in panic attacks this does not help, because there is no peril to run away from.

In fact, what it truly does is jeopardize your ability to think clearly and make wise decisions. Thus, the decisions that you make during a panic attack only contribute to worsening the symptoms. The second step in the AWARE method is just to wait and watch (or observe) your anxiety attack patterns. In the next section, I will discuss the importance of the two 'W' words.

Wait

The wait is to let the moment pass where you are incapable of thinking, remembering, or concentrating on things. Is it not also common in real life to think before acting? That saves us from making wrong decisions or doing things that could cause chaos.

Thus, after having accepted that you are having an anxiety attack, you need to wait for a little while. The waiting is similar to counting till ten when you are angry. The purpose of this step in AWARE is to buy you some time that may be required to gain back your ability to think.

You need to know that when people having severe symptoms of anxiety attacks tell you that they are doing this to themselves, they are not lying. Escalating or de-escalating the symptoms is slightly in your control. If you flee or make instant decisions, it will only cause you to struggle more.

Thus, no matter how fitting it may seem, delay the decision to leave the room that is making you anxious. There is another major thing to note here when I tell you to delay the fleeting tendency; it does not mean that you shut down the option of leaving altogether. This will make you feel trapped, the last thing you would want to bring upon yourself.

Keep the option open but do not just flee. Wait in the moment, and instead of fleeing in search of relief, let relief come to you by staying in the situation.

Watch

Watch the patterns, observe how your anxiety works, and in no time, you will realize that this is just a phase. There are ups and peaks, but at the same time, there is a low and an end. Observe how the anxiety is operating and causing you to act.

One of the best ways to watch your anxiety operate closely is by filling out a diary to keep records. Now to you, it may seem a little out of the blue kind of an idea, but there is ample proof that this method works. You are supposed to fill out a diary that includes questions related to your panic attack to help you get a closer look at how it works.

Filling out the diary during the attack is more beneficial than filling it out after the attack. The reasons for that are simple. Firstly, you do not miss out on any detail, and secondly, you now play the role of an observer rather than a victim. Do not confuse this to be a distraction as all the questions that you need to answer in the diary are all about the attack, but the role reversal to an observer lets you detach yourself from the heavy emotions just slightly and momentarily.

You can find these templates online as well as from any counselor. However, this raises another concern - what if I get an anxiety attack while I am on the road driving?

How Can You Achieve This Step if You Are in the Middle of Some Work?

Wait and watch is an ideal step for those who are the passive worker of a task, like a passenger in a car, a customer in a restaurant, or even a student in a class, but what happens when you are on the other side? When you are the person driving the task actively, then you need to continue doing it even if you are scared and almost frozen.

You cannot stop your car in the middle of a highway, can you? Thus, even though it is important to observe and even note down your reactions, you do not stop conducting your ongoing task. This is something that may require some assistance and practice, but you should learn to watch, wait and work.

Step 3: Anticipate and Take Actions

The previous two steps are perhaps the most crucial ones to follow in order to find some level of comfort during extreme anxiousness. Having known them, now you need to understand your role during an anxiety attack.

You are not the facilitator responsible for making the anxiety attack end. It will end eventually by itself, no matter what you decide or do. Even when you feel extremely scared and believe that it is never-ending, trust me, the anxiety will eventually pass. So, what are you supposed to do or responsible for, you ask?

You are responsible for trying your best to find some comfort for yourself. You can choose to flee the situation to make yourself struggle or you can make clear, rational decisions to ease out the fear, anxiousness, aches, and pains. If you feel helpless and are unable to relax or find comfort, then your job is to wait and let the storm pass.

The end of an anxiety attack is also a part of the attack and thus part of the process. To help you overcome and sail through the end, here are a few actions that most people find helpful as their attacks are nearing the end -

- **Silently Speak to Yourself -** Gently ask yourself the question - is there some danger that I am in? Or is it just a twinge? Respond to it by telling yourself that it is uncomfortable and that it is okay to be scared due to this. Tell yourself the realistic things, and it will help you to overcome the steep pain of the end.
- **Identify and Work with Your Body -** It is common for people to freeze when they are anxious. If you are someone who gets tense muscles, then realize that and try to gently relax those body parts. You need to relax your arms, legs, fingers, jaw, back, and shoulders slowly to not let the worse continue to reside in you.

- **Perform Abdominal or Belly Breathing -** Performing abdominal breathing (also known as diaphragmatic breathing) is a very commanding tool that helps overcome anxiety attacks. Take in and let out proper deep breaths, and it will relax you to a great extent.
- **Anchor Yourself to the Present -** Have you ever observed that you get a lot of "what if .." questions in your head during an anxiety attack? The reason for this is most of the time; people get anxious about what is to happen in the future. It is not happening to you at present; thus, to overcome or navigate through the phase, resume your current activity. Do things to keep you anchored in the present. You are in a store to shop. Resume shopping, look at a different product and its price, and ask questions to the storekeepers, and it will bring you back to reality. The reason to do this is when you get back to the present; the attack starts to subside.

Step 4: Repeat Your A-W-A's

The sad part about anxiety attacks is that you may feel better, and in the matter of minutes, you tend to get back the anxiety waves! People do not realize it and feel nothing worked and get even more anxious. This is when you should repeat all the above steps.

Please remember, it is a pattern. Your actions worked to ease you, but the anxiety came back, and that is normal. Repeat everything that you have done so far without worrying that this method is not working. It is working, and the step here itself is a reminder that anxiety comes in a wave, one after the other. So stay prepared and repeat your acceptance, wait and take action steps again and you will find comfort.

Step 5: Expect Brighter Rainbows

This is the last step and is for when the attack has almost or completely ended. You need to expect the best and realize that there are brighter rainbows at the end of the road. Whatever you were imagining is not going to come true.

All you have to do is wait and watch the best happen. The best that will happen is the reality, which will motivate you to remember that the danger you were anticipating is just a mirage and not the truth.

An anxiety attack is somewhat similar to extreme nervousness, the only difference being when you are having an anxiety attack, you tend to feel as if you are in danger. To give you a piece of peace, let me remind you that when you are in the middle of the road and a speeding car or bike is approaching you, your instant reaction is to try to escape from the front of the speeding vehicle as quickly as possible. Do you think instead of doing so, you would ever want to distract yourself? No!

This is just to help you get the idea that when you are trying to distract yourself, then the chances are that you are not in any real danger but overly anxious in the given circumstances or about a situation that is yet to happen or might not even occur. Keeping this in mind and practicing the A-W-A-R-E steps should help you to easily cope with mild panic attacks. Remember being mindful of the situation and accepting it, is the first and most important step to gradually stop these attacks from creeping back in abundantly.

Chapter 5: Stop the 'What If' Thoughts

When was the last time you had a terrible thought come into your mind which had absolutely no reason to be there? Or, how many times did you catch yourself feeling anxious today because of an intrusive thought that crept into your mind out of nowhere? If you can relate to this, do not be surprised because this is a common thing that happens to all of us. But what makes it worrisome is when it goes from being a one-time thing to something that happens every day and makes it difficult for us to function in our daily lives.

Yes, for some people, intrusive thoughts are not something they have to fight against just once in a while but regularly. And sometimes, it can get so bad that they may find themselves constantly bombarded with negative feelings and thoughts caused by their "what if" thoughts. If you are one of those people, I understand how eager you may be to learn how to get rid of them, but first, you must learn about the basics of what these "what if" thoughts are and how they affect you before you go any further.

What Are "What If" Thoughts?

Has it ever happened to you that right before an interview, you found yourself thinking, "What if I am not selected?" or "What if I make a fool out of myself?" If you have, then it would cheer you up to know that you are not alone. All of us, at one point or another, have experienced negative thoughts like these. And to be honest with you, it is not something you need to worry about. So you may be wondering what this chapter is all about. But hear me out. To a certain level, "What if" thoughts or intrusive thoughts are required because they serve a purpose. The purpose being it keeps you aware of the negative side of the picture, the things that could go wrong. Once you are aware of what could go wrong, you can try to do things in a way to ensure a positive outcome.

So intrusive thoughts sound like they are a good thing to have, right? But when these intrusive thoughts start to run uncontrolled in your mind, there begins the issue. But before we talk about how intrusive thoughts can harm a person, let us first identify them. So what exactly classifies a "what if" thought?

Here are some examples.

- "What if I fail the test?"
- "What if I lose my job?"
- "What if my girlfriend/boyfriend leaves me?"
- "What if my headache is a symptom of cancer?"
- "What if my family contacts Covid-19?"
- "What if I cannot pay this month's rent?"

You may notice that all of these statements have negative tones to them. This is something common with intrusive thoughts. They bring our deepest fears to the surface. And while it may seem harmless to have thoughts like these once a day, when it becomes incessant, and you cannot seem to perform even a simple task without being bombarded with such thoughts, it is a serious problem that you need to address and solve as soon as you can.

What Causes "What If" Thoughts?

Your brain is a massive network of thoughts. So it is completely normal for thoughts of all types to enter the brain at random times and leave just as quickly. It is the same with intrusive and "what if" thoughts. And they may or may not always have a cause for being there. Sometimes, these thoughts can be triggered due to multiple reasons. And people suffering from certain mental health conditions are more likely to experience negative "what if" thoughts than the rest. In such cases, intrusive thoughts act as symptoms of these disorders.

Sometimes the causes that can exaggerate intrusive thoughts are -

- ***High stress*** - People living or working in high-stress environments are more prone to experiencing negative thoughts as compared to those who do not.
- ***Obsessive-Compulsive Disorder (OCD)*** - People suffering from OCD often have a hard time dealing with intrusive thoughts that pop in and out of their heads frequently.
- ***Post Traumatic Stress Disorder (PTSD)*** - People suffering from PTSD often have intrusive thoughts related to their traumatic experiences. And any memories of the event can further escalate the negative cycle of thoughts.

But for most people who struggle with intrusive and negative "what if" thoughts, it is something that happens to them naturally and not as a symptom of any disorder.

Are "What If" Thoughts Harming Your Mental Health?

Our brains can be brilliant on their own, but at the same time, they are extremely quick to learn new things, which makes them very vulnerable if not given the right things to learn. Let me explain. Have you ever thought about why drinking alcohol once in a while is considered normal and fun while at the same time there are rehabilitation centers for people to help them quit drinking? It is because drinking in moderation is considered healthy, but when a person starts to cross the limit, it becomes unhealthy for them.

Similarly, even in the case of negative thoughts, while some people do not have a problem dealing with them once in a while, other people constantly worry themselves sick because of these "What if" thoughts.

Let us assume for a minute that you are living a normal day in your life, doing your usual things, but the entire time intrusive thoughts keep bothering you. For example, the minute you wake up in the morning, an intrusive thought comes into your head that says, "What if it is already 8 am, and I am late for work?" Although you know pretty well that it is only 6:10 am. And then, when you walk towards the kitchen to make yourself some breakfast, you think, "What if there is no milk?" Although you are aware that there is a gallon of milk in the fridge. Now imagine that this goes on for the rest of your day. How would that make you feel? Would you not feel frustrated at yourself and find it difficult to focus on even the simplest of tasks? This is what intrusive thoughts do to a person if it spirals out of control.

Especially for people who struggle with anxiety, depression, and stress, having frequent intrusive thoughts is extremely damaging. You may be aware that the basis on which an intrusive thought is built, is that of fear. The main purpose of an intrusive thought is to bring forward the worst thing that could happen to us in a situation. And for people who suffer from anxiety, you can only imagine what this extra dose of fear does. When a person suffers from anxiety, they are more likely than others to experience a crippling amount of fear and react to it through the fight or flight response. Now imagine the amount of negative effect the "what if" thoughts are going to have on such a person.

For people who struggle with depression, every day is a battle. And unless you have personally gone through it, you will not understand how difficult it is for them to even get up from bed every day and carry out their day-to-day activities. Now for someone like this, it is extremely detrimental to have intrusive thoughts kick into their minds at all times. And if these negative "what if" thoughts are not controlled, they can very quickly deteriorate their mental health even more, causing them to slip into a state of further depression and can even make them turn suicidal.

You know now that these kinds of thoughts can cause a person a huge amount of stress. Can you imagine what it can do to someone who already has a lot of stress in their life? It can cause them to become frustrated and even more stressed out than before. And if not taken care of, this high amount of stress can cause many health issues such as diabetes and high blood pressure. So you must keep your intrusive "what if" thoughts in check and work on them if they start interfering in your daily life.

Steps You Can Take to Get Rid of the "What If" Thoughts

Now that you are aware of all the reasons why intrusive thoughts are not good for you and why you must not let them spiral out of control, here are some ways you can get rid of them for good:

- ***Tune in to your thoughts*** - One of the mistakes we make which makes it easy for intrusive thoughts to creep into our heads is that we do not take a minute to think calmly about all the things that could go wrong, before we enter a situation. And instead of making ourselves aware of the negatives of a situation, we just allow our "what if" thoughts to do that for us. And when it happens, we are faced with sadness, stress, anger, and frustration. So instead of waiting for the "what if" thoughts to show themselves, you should tune in to your thoughts before you get into a situation. One of the ways you can do this is by asking yourself, "What is the worst thing that can happen right now?" Once you ask yourself this, you will see that the answers that pop up in your mind are much less harmful than the negative "what if" thoughts.

- ***Remind yourself that you can handle even the worst situation with ease*** - Once you have thought about the worst scenario, you should always remind yourself that no matter the negative consequences, you will be able to handle them effectively. Think about it, if you are struggling with a thought like "What if I lose my job?" Then your response to that should be, "Then I will find a better job." You will find that by doing this, your negative thoughts quickly disappear, and your feeling of frustration is replaced by a feeling of optimism. I know that it may be challenging to convince yourself that no matter how difficult things become, you will be able to handle them. However, you should constantly look for strategies to convince yourself that you can. Often when we are stressed, we fail to view the options in front of us. So always remember that every time you feel anxious or stressed over an intrusive thought, you do not see the complete picture, and there may be many ways for you to overcome the situation which you are currently unable to see.

- ***Think of what could go right*** - The primary reason we fall prey to our "what if" thoughts is that we allow them to paint us a picture of absolute horror, without realizing that this is not the truth. Intrusive thoughts are only negative thoughts that wander inside your head for too long and make you feel sad and worried. But what we often forget is that thoughts are not reality and the picture intrusive thoughts paint to us is not the truth. There is always the chance that what we fear the most, may never happen to us. You may never lose your job. You may never fail the test, be evicted from your apartment, or suffer from a deadly disease. Do not let your intrusive thoughts make you believe that it is a reality. And you can do so by thinking about all the things that could go right when you are dealing with a situation. So instead of thinking, "What if I lose my job?" Try to replace it with, "What if my boss praises me today for my hard work?" See how quickly you can change your mindset from a negative to a positive one? Try to practice this every time you find an intrusive thought bothering you.

- ***Consider taking therapy*** - If you still are unable to get rid of these negative thoughts using the above-mentioned steps, you should consider taking therapy. A professional therapist will treat your intrusive thoughts with cognitive-behavioral therapy (CBT). In this type of therapy, you will be taught different ways of thinking, which will help you become less sensitive to your intrusive thoughts. And in controlled settings, your therapist may also consider exposing you to certain triggers to change your ways of reacting to them and help you regulate your emotions and actions when faced with triggers.

- ***Taking medication if required*** - As explained earlier, having frequent intrusive thoughts are sometimes a symptom of mental health disorders like OCD, PTSD, and high stress. Mental health disorders cannot be treated without proper medication, and hence it would be impractical to expect you to stop overthinking and allowing the "What if" thoughts to ruin your day if you are struggling with mental health issues. In this case, you must take proper medications to treat your mental health disorder. Because if your intrusive thoughts are a result of your mental illness, they cannot be treated with the above-mentioned steps, and it will require much more than that to stop them from becoming recurrent and break the cycle. For those of you who have tried everything and still feel like there is no improvement, you should consider getting a clinical diagnosis of why you continue to struggle with intrusive thoughts and talk to a professional who can help solve your problem. And once you get the necessary help, you will find that your life has become much easier, and your "What if" thoughts do not bother you as much as before.

- ***Practicing self-love and self-care*** - With everything said, it is equally important that you practice self-love at all stages of your healing and growth. Love is a very powerful motivator. So instead of feeling angry or upset at yourself for allowing intrusive thoughts to ruin your day, try to practice kindness and forgive yourself for your thoughts. It is also important that you learn to separate yourself from your thoughts and not make thoughts your identity. Always remember that thoughts are abstract things, and they are neither the truth nor any sort of a prediction of what is going to happen. So learn to treat them like mere thoughts. Very similar to any other thought that comes to your head. Learn to watch them as they come and learn to let them go without allowing yourself to pay much attention to them.

By following the above steps, you can effectively avoid letting negative "what if" thoughts stress you out and affect your mental health. So remember to use them every time you find yourself facing an intrusive thought.

Intrusive thoughts or the "What if" thoughts may appear harmless at first, but they can quickly become your biggest enemy if not taken care of and managed at the right time. Learning how to effectively handle intrusive thoughts may be difficult, but you can make peace with them and stop them from negatively affecting you with practice and dedication.

Chapter 6: Cognitive Distortion in Depression

"I performed so poorly in front of all the managers. I'm nothing more than a failure. Now, I can even lose this project."

Have you ever noticed when you are facing failure or feeling depressed that you have random negative thoughts? Negative thoughts just keep popping in our heads whenever something goes wrong, don't they? Yes, and it happens all the time. From the moment you start worrying, your mind builds up various speculative thoughts in your head. Most of the time, these are just *ifs-and-but* situations that you think in your mind could have or should have happened instead of what *actually* happened. This is your mind trying to tell you where you performed the mistake and what you could or should have done instead. These thoughts fill your mind with negativity, and you get more depressed, which leads to more thoughts, and the cycle goes on and on. We often find ourselves caught up in this repetitive spiral of negative self-criticism and loathing.

But, do you know what this is called? It is a form of *cognitive distortion.* These thoughts and beliefs that randomly keep popping in your head are the cognitive distortions at work. Usually, any belief, perception, or thoughts that are inaccurate and give rise to negative feelings can be termed cognitive distortions. Every one of us experiences such distortions in our life, but those living with depression know them all *too* well. If you start facing these distortions very frequently in your life, they can become problematic. Having too many cognitive distortions can increase your various health issues like having more anxiety, stress, depression, and other negative behaviors.

But, don't worry. We've got you covered. In this chapter, we will go through cognitive distortion in *more* detail. You will get to know the most common types of cognitive distortions and how you can recognize such thinking patterns in yourself to prevent them from repeating in the future.

Before we begin, let us first discuss how cognitive distortions are connected with your mental health.

What Are Cognitive Distortions?

In psychological terms, cognitive distortions are any form of exaggerated, false, inaccurate, or irrational thought that you might have. And we all face them in our lives at some point or another. But, usually, these thoughts and beliefs occur more often when you are depressed or stressed.

If your mind constantly disturbs you with thoughts like "I'm a failure," "I can never get this right," or "No one will ever love me," it becomes very hard to stay positive. We often chastise ourselves whenever any bad things happen. Our feelings follow our thinking patterns, and negative thoughts from failures are known to harbor depression.

I'm sure you realize why these thoughts are called 'distortions'? It is because all these thoughts that you are visualizing are *actually* not happening! They are simply *made up* by your mind as a response to the events that did not go the way you wanted. They are just false thoughts trying to trap you into endless depression by *distorting* the actual reality. If you start thinking of something every now and then, you might actually start believing it to be true, and our emotions and feelings closely follow our beliefs.

Cognitive distortions are closely related to automatic negative thought patterns, cognitive errors, and maladaptive thoughts and behavior. Depression and anxiety can easily lead you into habitual negative thoughts, but in many cases, cognitive distortions actually lead to depression. It works in both ways.

What Are the Most Common Types of Cognitive Distortions?

Do you know how many types of cognitive distortions there are? Can you try thinking of a few?

You probably won't believe me, but there are several types of distortions that can affect your thought patterns. Initially, it was believed to be only six, but now we know of nearly 17 types of distortions that people normally face in their daily lives. Don't you want to know what these are? Learning about them, especially the most common ones, can help you recognize them early – the moment they pop up in your head. So, keep reading!

Overgeneralization

Have you ever considered one specific situation as the norm and assumed all other events to be the same? If so, then you are overgeneralizing. It is the type of cognitive distortion that makes you take an isolated case and apply what happened there to all other subsequent situations. Your mind does not let you consider your current situation as something different and forces you to assume that everything will happen *exactly* the same way as it did in the past.

Here's an example. Let's say you do not have a pretty face and spend most of your time at home. Your one close friend asks you to step outside and make more friends, but you feel it's useless because someone has called you ugly before. And, now you think that *similarly*, everyone else will also call you ugly and that you will *always* remain 'ugly.'

Two people are never the same, and if anyone ever dislikes you, that doesn't mean that everyone else will too. By assuming that, you are overgeneralizing and building a wall between you and the world. When people overgeneralize, their minds usually do not consider all the other possibilities. The mind focuses on one negative feeling and turns it into a rule. If you're thinking of sentences having the words – 'always' or 'never' – you can recognize it as overgeneralization.

Mind Reading

Did you ever think that you are a mind reader, that you can guess beforehand what other people are going to say? Mind you, we inadvertently think that we can read others' minds, but we cannot. In fact, it is another form of cognitive distortion, where you assume what others are thinking and that they are thinking something negative about you. But that doesn't always hold true.

Mind reading thoughts are easy to identify. You are most likely mind reading if your thoughts align with patterns like–

- "They are all staring at me. I must have said something incorrect."
- "He is not speaking to me. I must have hurt him."

In reality, most people are simply focused on their lives and actions. So, even if they are staring at you, they might be only thinking about what they would do if they were in your place. You can also refer to mind reading as '*jumping to conclusions.*'

Emotional Reasoning

In emotional reasoning, you try to decide the truth of a matter based on how you feel about it. Here, your emotions control your actions and dictate your reasoning. You start believing in something because your emotions tell you to, rather than analyzing it with proper reasoning.

You are facing this cognitive distortion if you are thinking something like -

- “I am afraid of that place. It must be dangerous.”
- "I am feeling hopeless. Maybe I am really hopeless."
- “The room is too untidy. It’s hopeless if I try to clean it.”

You might find a task too *tedious*, but is it really hopeless? In fact, you can clean your house with little effort. However, you try to conclude the matter just because the task looked too uphill. Although you should acknowledge your emotions, you can’t let them rule over you. Feeling about something in a certain manner doesn’t make it actually true. If a situation feels *overwhelming*, don’t listen to your negative thoughts. Divide the task into smaller parts and *prioritize* the one that seems most important. It is not important to reach the target then and there. What is important is that you actually take *some* steps to at least reach the target.

All-or-Nothing Thinking

This cognitive distortion is also called ‘*black-and–white*’ thinking, dichotomous thinking, or polarized thinking. Here, you basically try to interpret everything in either of the two extremely opposite perspectives – totally good or totally bad. In this type of thinking, you are likely to use absolute words like ‘forever,’ ‘always,’ and ‘never.’ You either classify the cat as black or white, cute or ugly, but nothing in between.

Let's see an example. Suppose you applied for a newly arrived project in your company. However, the manager decided to assign it to someone else because of their higher experience. But, you very much wanted to do it, and so now you start feeling that you will *no longer* receive any project and will *always* remain a failure.

In life, hardly anything is ever *completely* absolute. There are and will be grey areas everywhere. You should try to remove all these *absolute* thoughts from your mind and accept everything as they are, not in terms of '*totally good*' or '*totally bad.*' It might be true that you do not yet have the qualification or experience to handle such a project, but that doesn't mean that you don't have the experience to do any project.

Personalization

Here, you start to take things *personally* and blame yourself for all the negative events, assuming that you are the one who caused them. Even if something is not your fault, you start holding yourself accountable, assuming that it was your *responsibility*.

Suppose your son is performing poorly at school. So, you start thinking that it is all your fault and that he isn't studying because of you. But is it actually so?

You can only advise and guide your son; the rest is up to him. It is he who has to study and pass his exams. He is responsible for his actions, not you. Stop holding yourself responsible for every matter, especially when you have no hand in it. On the contrary, would you hold yourself creditable if your son achieved the best grades? No, right? Your son achieved those grades through his own hard work. Similarly, why hold yourself at fault when they fail?

Should Statements

Often you may have felt that you *should* have done a particular work in a different way – painted it using a different color or used a different medium, haven't you? Well, these are again a form of cognitive distortions, and we call them '*should statements*.' Here, you start filling your mind with self-talk that mostly comprises thoughts lined with words - '*should have*' or '*shouldn't have*.'

- "I shouldn't have said it like that."
- "I should have completed my assignments before the due date."
- "I ought to devote my time towards my family."

We only *bother* ourselves by thinking that what we have done isn't playing out right, and instead, we *should* have opted for the other solution. But, just accept it; they are not that way and cannot be changed. Thinking about matters from this perspective will only make you feel more resentful and make it harder for you to accept things as they are.

Even if you intend to motivate yourself with 'should statements,' they only turn out to fuel your sense of guilt and elevate *unattainable expectations*. Your mind thinks of such statements to force you to fulfill your expectations, but when you fail, you end up feeling guilty and dejected, as if you have failed.

So, next time you decide to motivate yourself, avoid using words like 'must,' 'should,' 'have to,' or 'ought.'

Disqualifying the Positives

When you disqualify the positives, you try to negate anything that is good. When you are presented with two situations - one good and one bad – you reject the positive situation completely as if it never happened or it only happened by sheer luck. In fact, even if something good happens to you or you perform something well, instead of acknowledging it and taking the credit, you attribute it to other people.

Let's say a photographer takes a picture of your face. After printing, your friend looks at the picture and exclaims that you look gorgeous in it. You simply brush aside her compliment and reply back that the photographer must have brightened your complexion because you never look so good in real life.

But what if it is actually true? What if you actually look good and the photographer did not edit your photo? Don't refuse to accept the positives in life. This type of thinking can only *lower* your self-esteem and make you lose confidence in yourself and your abilities. There may come a time when you start doubting your own capabilities and admit defeat even before trying. Start appreciating the small compliments that you receive with a smile and see how your life turns around like magic!

Catastrophizing

This cognitive distortion is also termed '*magnification and minimization*.' Here, either you are *exaggerating* something or *underestimating* the possibility of its occurrence. So, what kind of people do this? People who have a habit of minimizing their success and magnifying their failures.

Suppose you have been given ten sums to solve, of which the last sum is the hardest. You solved nine sums, including the last one, which was praiseworthy because only a few students were able to solve it, including you. However, when your friend congratulates you for solving it, you diminish it by saying that you ought to have practiced harder for missing the moderate sum and that the solution of the last sum came by luck.

If it has become one of your habits, then what can you do to prevent this from happening? You should not let your mind only filter out the negative thoughts. If you get bogged down by one of your mistakes, you may not see the clear picture again. Remember the old adage – "He can't see the forest for the trees"? One mistake cannot make you an overnight failure, nor will it make you a terrible friend. And when you're depressed, you need to have great companions. – both others and also yourself.

How Can We Prevent Cognitive Distortions?

If you sit down and start analyzing your cognitive distortions with depression, you will realize that they form a *vicious* and unending cycle. If you're thinking of negative thoughts all the time, it can lead you to depression, which can further increase the severity of the negative thoughts. And so, the cycle keeps repeating itself with no obvious conclusion or beginning.

But, you don't have to listen to all the inappropriate things that your mind tries to pop into your head that are untrue. You need to fight off the evil voices that speak in your head and try to pull you into the trap of complete depression. In this battle, you yourself are the biggest enemy that you need to defeat.
By now, you must have realized how destructive cognitive distortions can be and why you should not let them have free rein over your mind. To do so, you have to learn how to change your way of thinking. Yes, it will take time and a little effort. But, with continued practice and persistence, you will find yourself turning a new leaf with a positive mindset.

So what are the steps towards attaining a positive and happy way of thinking? How can you turn your negative school of thought into a train of positive vibes and energy?

Recognize Cognitive Distortions

If you can already recognize when you are facing these cognitive distortions, trust me, you already have crossed a long distance. And, those of you who haven't been able to identify when and how you are facing these cognitive distortions, take your time and find them.

After finding out the causes, try remembering the automatic responses that you took. Practice identifying these responses in your head. Is there any way to accomplish this in an easier process?

Yes, you can always try out strategies like *journaling* and *mindfulness* to help you strengthen your self-consciousness and make you more aware of your thoughts and actions. Mindfulness helps you to focus your mind on the present situation, this can help you see how your way of thinking is affecting your feelings and emotions. Journaling, on the other hand, can help you spot the recurring patterns that give rise to anxiety, stress, and depression within you. With these, you can learn more about your cognitive distortions and how you need to fight them.

Alter Your Thinking

After you can clearly identify by yourself any cognitive distortion that you currently face, you can start practicing a different way of thinking – one that is more *positive* and *enthusiastic*. Gather your thoughts and reframe them in a way that would encourage you, instead of belittling you.

Have you heard of *cognitive reframing*? It's a strategy that helps you try out a *new perspective* of how you see the various events, relationships, or situations completely differently. For example, instead of jumping to conclusions or imagining the worst possible case at the very beginning, you can reframe the situation by considering *alternative* explanations. Believe me, it helps.

Seek Professional Help

If you cannot control the severity of your negative thoughts or you are becoming more depressed whenever you start thinking about rectifying those thoughts, you can always seek professional advice. You can talk to a mental health expert about your cognitive distortion problems and listen to what they have to say. A therapist will help you recognize your distortions and work you through processes like *cognitive restructuring* to alter your thought patterns and form a new positive mindset.

You can also go for *cognitive behavioral therapy* (CBT) upon their advice. It has shown considerable success in helping people manage the train of negative thoughts that automatically arrive in their mind and therefore reduce the chances of falling into depression. If you feel that you need help, don't be afraid; always consult with a doctor.

Your therapist can also guide you as to how you can develop new coping skills, strengthen your personal relationships, and practice relaxation techniques to calm your mind and prevent it from racing away with negative thoughts. All of them can improve your way of thinking and enhance your well-being.

Recognizing your cognitive distortions is the doorway to positive thinking and a better life. Unless you challenge yourself to try and become positive, you cannot escape from these distortions. Try changing your thought pattern and see how your mood lifts off! Always remember you *are* what you think yourself to be!

Chapter 7: Practice Meditation and Mindfulness

Ok, so now that you know what anxiety is and how it combines with stress to give rise to negative thoughts and cognitive distortions, you are probably also curious to know how you can prevent them. Don't worry; we have the solution, and we're going to look at it in this chapter itself.

But, before we do that, let's quickly recap what we learned in the previous chapters about depression and how it can affect your mental health.

A Quick Recap: What Is Depression? How does It Affect You?

Depression is a mood disorder that causes a *persistent* and, in most cases, *overwhelming* feeling of sadness accompanied by a significant lack of interest and motivation to pursue your daily activities. When depression persists for a long time, it causes *serious* physical and mental ailments which, if left untreated, can become fatal. Even though most symptoms of depression are physical, the disorder actually originates in your brain.

Depression is one of the most common mental health problems across the world. It's not only the most common mental illness, but it's also one of the most tenacious. For many people, depression is a lifelong battle. Nearly 80 percent of people in the whole world who have experienced bouts of depression at least once in their life may relapse back into it.

According to the World Health Organization (WHO), more than 264 million people around the world suffer from various forms of depression. Do you know that in America alone, more than 17.3 million people have undergone at least one episode of depression?

So, what happens when you are depressed? How do your brain and mind react to prolonged stress and negativity?

- ***Your brain has difficulty controlling your mood and emotions.*** Scientists have determined that depression reduces the size of the part of the brain that is responsible for regulating our mood and emotions. The regions which are mostly affected by depression are the *hippocampus*, *amygdala*, *frontal*, and *prefrontal cortices*. You suffer from stress and anxiety mostly when your hippocampus and amygdala regions shrink. With smaller frontal and prefrontal cortices, your impulse control is negatively impacted, and you find it hard to control your emotions.
- ***A lack of neurotransmitters negatively affects your thoughts and feelings.*** In

normal conditions, your healthy brain has a *delicate* balance of special brain chemicals called neurotransmitters. Depression disrupts your brain's normal state and creates a chemical imbalance marked by low neurotransmitter functioning. When your serotonin levels drop significantly, you start feeling tired, anxious, and sad very often. Similarly, low levels of norepinephrine and dopamine make you feel exhausted and uninterested in activities that you enjoyed previously.

- ***Your brain does not receive an adequate amount of oxygen to function properly.*** As a result, you start exhibiting various symptoms associated with memory and mood. The shortage of oxygen causes your brain to function *below* the optimal level, thereby making it unable to make the right decisions at the proper time. Your reaction time and response rate fall significantly, leaving you confused, uninterested, irritated, and annoyed.

If you ask a doctor or a mental health expert, they will probably ask you to take medications and undergo therapy to cure your depressed mind. Drugs can lose their effectiveness over time, if they even work at all. Such is the power of depression. But is the prolonged intake of anti-depressant drugs good for your health?

Did you know that many of these medications have their own side effects, which can make you completely depend on them to maintain your normal happiness for your entire life? If you miss your daily dose, you start to feel irritated and restless and ultimately become agitated and frustrated. So, is there an alternate way to treat depression without resorting to such addictive anti-depressant drugs? Yes, obviously there are, but not many people know about it!

Did you know that you can cure depression using *meditation* and *mindfulness*? After performing significant research in the past few decades, experts have found that mindfulness and regular meditation can help you relieve depression by changing the way your brain answers to calls of anxiety and stress. Studies suggest that *mindfulness-based cognitive therapy* is more effective than medication in preventing depression relapse among people who have a history of suffering from recurring bouts of depression. It is also able to reduce depressive symptoms in people who are presently active with depression.

Have you heard of 'mindfulness' and 'meditation' before? Or do they sound completely new to you? Let's look at them in more detail.

What Is Mindfulness?

You can define mindfulness as our inherent ability to be fully present and aware of what is happening around us and what we are doing. It means to stay calm and composed in any given situation. When you are mindful, you don't unnecessarily over-react or become overwhelmed by what is happening around you.

Even though it is a basic human ability that we all possess, you can't be mindful unless you practice it on a daily basis! Whenever you are bringing awareness to all your actions that you are performing through your senses, or making your mind aware of your present emotions and thoughts, you're actually exhibiting mindfulness.

What can you achieve by being mindful? The goal of mindfulness is to become aware of the various mental, physical, and emotional processes that are going on in our bodies. When you are trying to be mindful, you are actually trying to grasp how your mind works internally.

How Mindfulness Helps You Relieve Depression?

By being mindful, you are actually trying to focus on building your awareness of your feelings and sensations at that moment without trying to understand, interpret, or judge them in any way. To put it simply, when you are mindful, you're *retraining* your brain to prevent it from getting overwhelmed by whatever's happening around you. By learning how to be fully present and aware of what you're experiencing without becoming over-reactive or overwhelmed, you can considerably reduce your stress and anxiety, which are the driving factors of depression.

You can also refer to mindfulness as *'thought detachment.'* You imagine your thoughts as clouds drifting in the sky or leaves floating on the water's surface, and practice not to engage them or become attached to them.

Did you know that mindfulness helps restore the brain's control over your emotions? In your brain, you have a region called the medial prefrontal cortex (mPFC), which is also known as the *'me center'* and is responsible for processing all the information regarding yourself. It also processes the worries you have about your future and your obsessions from the past.

Scientists have discovered that due to depression, your medial prefrontal cortex and amygdala become over-activated. When you experience lots of stress, your mPFC goes into overdrive and alerts the amygdala (the *'fear center'*) to trigger the fight-or-flight response mode in your body. The two parts of your brain interlock with one another and forms an overwhelming cycle that causes depression. Mindfulness helps you to prevent these two parts from interlocking.

What Is Meditation?

To simply put, meditation is all about *exploring*! In meditation, there is no fixed destination. You don't sit down to meditate thinking of completing some task or achieving your goal. It's about you exploring all about yourself in those few minutes.

When you meditate, you set out on a journey to explore the depths of your mind – all the sensations that you feel (the air gently blowing on your skin or the sound of music coming from outside), the emotions that you experience (love, hate, resent, or crave), and thoughts that come across your mind.

In meditation, you suspend all your other physical activities and start concentrating on the working of your mind and understand the flow of energy within your body. You try to *free* your mind and prevent it from getting distracted by any external activities.

How Can Meditation Boost Up Your Mental Health?

Meditation may not be able to disappear all the symptoms of depression, but it can surely help you manage them. Meditation helps you to respond to stress and anxiety in a different way. It prevents your medial prefrontal cortex from going into overdrive and suppresses the triggers that are stimulated from this region and the amygdala. So, do you understand now why your stress levels fall when you meditate?

Meditation protects the hippocampus.
The hippocampus portion of your brain is responsible for storing your memories and learning new things. Daily meditation for about fifteen minutes can significantly increase the number of grey cells in this area. Do you know that people affected by depression have a smaller hippocampus than normal people?

It changes your way of thinking.
With depression, lots of negative thoughts start filling up your mind. You start criticizing yourself harshly over every matter and paint yourself in a negative light. You often feel mad at yourself and start detesting life. Meditation doesn't necessarily block or push your negative thoughts and feelings away. Rather, it helps you to look at them from a different viewpoint in a calm and collected manner and accept them as they are without over-reacting.

Meditation helps you attain mindfulness.
Whenever you meditate, you start rationalizing all your thoughts and feelings based on your present situation. You judge your actions with a clear mind. It helps your mind to regain its control over your thoughts and feelings. With regular meditation, you start practicing your mind to become more aware of all our actions, which in turn helps to create mindfulness.

It prepares your mind to face stressful situations.
If there's an important day at your office, meditating for ten to fifteen minutes in the morning can help you relieve the nervousness and stress that you are facing. It shifts the mind's focus from answering your stress calls to a state of calm. Meditation helps you to refrain from acting upon the thoughts and feelings which you don't like. Instead, you calmly accept that even if those thoughts affect you, they don't necessarily change who you are. As you let go of these thoughts while you are meditating, the negative and vicious cycle of stress and anxiety is broken.

Meditation Techniques That Can Help You Treat Depression

Now that you know how meditation can help you fight off depression, it's time to look at some of the best meditation techniques that can help you with the process. Practicing these meditation techniques regularly, can help you think more clearly and have a calmer mind, which will help you tackle all your day's stress and worries!

1. ***Visualization*** – When you focus your mind on some pleasant images or replay your happy memories, your mind becomes calm. If you had negative thoughts in your mind earlier, you forget them after you meditate and end up with happy thoughts.
2. ***Loving-kindness meditation*** – By creating a kind and lovable environment for yourself, you remove the scope of generating any doubt or self-criticism. You learn to combat your negative emotions, hopelessness, and low self-esteem using this technique.
3. ***Chanting*** – This form of meditation helps activate the parts of your brain which are responsible for mood regulation and emotion

control. It is also sometimes known as transcendental meditation.

4. ***Mindfulness meditation*** – It is the most potent form of meditation, and all the other forms are mostly derived from it. It makes you aware of your actions and surroundings by making you live yourself to the fullest at any given moment.
5. ***Breath awareness meditation*** – This form focuses on your breathing and helps regulate your blood flow in accordance with your breathing pattern. It helps you tackle your challenging emotions and reduces the cortisol levels to ease your anxiety.
6. ***Yoga*** – When you combine meditation with yoga, you enhance not only your mental well-being but also your breathing techniques, physical postures, and various other things.
7. ***Body scan meditation*** – Here, you try to focus on different parts of your body one at a time. As you move from one part to the other, you inhale and exhale accordingly to allow your mind to concentrate on the portion you are currently focusing on. Your mind becomes

aware of what each part of your body is doing currently and learns to feel different emotions without reacting automatically in response.

How Can You Become Mindful Throughout the Day?

I'm sure you have noticed that most of the time, when you regret your decisions or feel ashamed of your actions, it is when your body acts on its own from your emotions. Almost as if you are a puppet in the hands of your thoughts and emotions!

Wouldn't it be wonderful if there was a buffer between your thoughts and your automatic responses? Like if you didn't always react the way you did but had some time to think before your body acted? I bet you do.

Mindfulness helps you achieve just that. It puts some space between you and your immediate reactions and helps break down those conditioned responses. But, for you to become really mindful, you have to start practicing it daily at every moment, no matter what work you do.

But is it really possible? Can you truly practice mindfulness at every moment without getting distracted? Absolutely! The only thing you need is some regular practice. Here's how you can tune into mindfulness from the morning to the night.

- ***Set aside some time*** – You don't need a separate room, bench, cushion, or any special equipment to meditate daily. The only thing you require to develop your mindfulness is some space and time in your daily schedule.

- ***Closely observe the present moment*** – If you want to be mindful, you can't shut your mind off from whatever is happening around you. Your goal should not be to block whatever is happening around you from entering your mind or quieting your thoughts and emotions. Instead, it is completely the opposite. You simply need to pay attention to every detail that is happening around you without reacting to it. Yes, you can't speak or act in response! More difficult than it sounds, don't you think?
- ***Ignore your judgments*** – You can't react in any way. So, even if you strongly feel the urge to tell or perform something, just ignore it. Just fine-tune your mind to let go of every judgment that arises in your mind. It is like a promise that you made to yourself. Failing it will only defeat the purpose.
- ***Return to your observations*** – The tensest moments will arise whenever your

mind makes a judgment, and you feel like reacting to it. If you can successfully steer yourself through this tumultuous time, you are nearer to mastering mindfulness than ever before. Don't let your mind lose focus. Losing your concentration will give your mind the opportunity to return back to your older self. You cannot let this happen by any means. Our minds often get carried away in thought, and we lose focus for that small period. This is why mindfulness is so important! It is the practice of giving a deaf ear to all the judgments in your mind and staying in the present moment at all times by returning again and again whenever the train of thoughts arrive.

- ***Don't be harsh on your mind*** – It may so happen that initially, you find it extremely difficult to maintain complete focus in the present, and your mind may wander away once or twice. What you need to do in this situation is not to criticize or rebuke yourself, but gently stop the train of thoughts in its tracks and bring your mind back to the present. Don't judge your mind for whatever thoughts come to your mind. Be kind to your mind even if it wanders. Just keep recognizing whenever such instances happen and bring your mind back.

That's the process. It might sound simple and easy to follow, but you can take my word for it; it isn't so. The mantra is to keep performing this over and over again. You may not get the results immediately, but with time, they are bound to come.

The key to overcoming depression is never to lose hope. Believing in yourself and in your strength to overcome failure will help you survive through the rough waters. With meditation, you can overcome the negative feelings and thoughts that start popping in your head randomly whenever you are dejected.

The trick is to make your mind focus on one positive thing and relax whenever the negative emotions come knocking at the door. Choose any of the above meditation techniques that you feel will work the best for you, and make sure to implement them in your routine. Mindfulness is something that you can't attain overnight or if you don't practice daily. You need to keep reminding yourself about your surroundings to help your mind become completely aware of your present situation. And meditation can help you achieve that.

The most dangerous form of depression is the one that pulls people back into it. It normally happens to people who ignore the seriousness of the issue and leave it as it is. They think of it as only something that is momentary. Relapses are very dangerous and can leave you depressed forever if you don't start preparing yourself to fight them. People who run the risk of depression are dealing with lots of negative thoughts, emotions, feelings, and beliefs bottled up inside them. It's easier for such people to fall into a depressive relapse at any time.

By attaining mindfulness, you can prevent your mind from stepping into the territory of negative emotions and thoughts. Believe me; it's easier said than done. Achieving mindfulness is not some piece of cake that every person can master. Only if you're willing to commit yourself completely to it with the right conviction, only then can you attain mindfulness. Just remember the saying – "*Hard work always pays off.*"

Chapter 8: Dealing With the Cycle of Perfectionism

People, who are perfectionists, always tend to set unrealistic and unachievable goals. Then when they fail to achieve these goals, they get stressed or depressed! This is a never-ending cycle that is extremely unhealthy and dangerous for one's mental health! The vicious cycle of perfectionism goes somewhat like this -

- Suddenly you get a lot of motivation to do a particular thing, and you just can't sit back unless you are doing it.
- You have a feeling that it is a do-or-die situation. You feel like either you should do it well or not do it at all!
- You get this insatiable drive to make everything perfect that you forget focusing on the little progress you made and start criticizing yourself for the slightest flaws.
- You push yourself so hard that you almost forget to care about yourself and burn yourself out in the process.
- Then you start feeling overwhelmed and stuck. You don't seem to find a solution and

everything seems to fall apart! You feel like you have failed yourself and everyone in the process.

- Then suddenly, after being depressed for a few days, you get re-motivated and repeat the same cycle all over again!

When this gets ingrained in our brain, it gets very difficult to get out! But if we follow a few things consciously, then we can help the situation to a great extent. Keep reading to find out about the things that need to be done in order to deal with the vicious cycle of perfectionism.

Being Aware of Your Tendencies

Awareness is the most important thing when it comes to healing from something. If you don't know what you need to heal, then no matter how hard you try, you are never going to be able to heal yourself from it. So, the first thing that you need to do is understand your patterns and tendencies. Accept the fact that you are doing something unhealthy over and over again, which is extremely detrimental to your mental health. Take out some time, sit back, and try to pay attention to your thinking patterns related to perfectionism. To understand them better, you can even try writing them down somewhere. It will help you get a better understanding of the overall situation. If we don't know the disease, how will we cure it? Once we are completely aware of our thought patterns and how it harms us, we will be able to figure out ways to handle them!

Focusing on the Positives

People have a tendency to always focus on the negatives, which is not at all okay! We are often too harsh on ourselves, and we don't even realize it. We tell ourselves horrible things that we would probably never tell others! Criticizing ourselves on every little thing is not going to do any good! If you think that it will help you to improve, you are totally wrong! It is only going to bring our morale down and make the entire process sufferable and miserable. If you want everything to be perfect, it doesn't necessarily mean that you have to continuously fixate on the negative parts. It is very important to recognize the little signs of progress and appreciate them. Only that will give you the motivation to progress further. So, if you are unsatisfied with a particular thing, take note of that and motivate yourself to do better instead of criticizing yourself. Celebrate the small victories so as to remember how far you have come and what it means to you!

Allowing Yourself to Make Mistakes and Accept It

Everybody makes mistakes. Making mistakes is as common as anything! Nobody is perfect, and nobody can do everything perfectly. When you are working for something, there will always be a few things that are going wrong or are not going to go the way you planned them to! That doesn't mean all your efforts have gone in vain or you have worked for nothing. If you are someone who thinks like that, stop it! Learn to accept your mistakes and rectify them. If you look into things with a positive approach, then things will be pretty easy for you to rectify and improve. Don't ignore your mistakes, but also don't be too demotivated when you make one! Try to see where you are going wrong and then make the necessary changes in order to correct it and not repeat that again. Mistakes are sometimes important because that is how we learn, and that is how we improve. Failure is the pillar of success- it's a popular proverb that we should never forget!

Setting More Reasonable Goals

The most common mistake that all perfectionists make is that they set unrealistic goals which are unachievable most of the time. And when they finally fail to achieve those goals, for obvious reasons, they tend to get stressed, anxious, and depressed. This is a very unhealthy thought pattern that you must change! You need to understand that it isn't a good idea to set an unrealistic and unachievable goal in the first place. You can't expect to start your journey and then reach the epitome in one go! That is an absurd thought and should never be encouraged at any cost. Set small achievable goals. Take one step at a time! When you set a small target, and you achieve it, the happiness and the sense of satisfaction that you get is unexplainable. And only that will give you the motivation to push yourself further and do better things. So, appreciate all the small victories, acknowledge how far you have come, look into the mistakes and where you went wrong, take notes and proceed further. This is the only correct way to break the loop of perfectionism and depression and come out victorious.

Learning How to Receive Criticism

Another mistake that perfectionists make is that they can't handle criticism! If you are someone who gets passive-aggressive and defensive when someone criticizes your work or something about you, then you need to stop doing that. Because that will only give you stress and anxiety and will hamper your work even more. If you see that someone is constantly criticizing your work, no matter what you do, and that they are doing it only to disturb your mental peace, you should ignore them! But some people criticize you out of genuine concern, and it is your duty to identify and recognize these people. Constructive criticism is actually very important for you as it is the only way you can identify the mistakes others see in your work, that you are unable to see yourself. Successful people always welcome constructive criticism with an open heart because they know that is the only way they can succeed. So, whenever someone criticizes you constructively or gives you a piece of advice, make sure to hear them out, analyze it and check if they have any other intention or not, and then work accordingly. If you realize that they are doing it out of genuine concern, thank them and rectify your work. It is only going to make you better and closer to your goals!

Trying to Put Less Pressure on Yourself

Another common mistake that perfectionists make is pushing themselves too hard. Perfectionists want everything to be perfect, so they sometimes overwork and burn themselves out in the process of ensuring everything goes "perfectly." If you are someone who does this, stop doing that because it will be harmful to you in the long run. Don't put so much pressure on yourself that you will break down in the middle of your journey. But that doesn't mean that you will sit back and relax all the time. Putting pressure is fine, but not too much! Push yourself to work hard and always keep yourself motivated to work towards your goals. Also, take breaks and celebrate your growth. If you can't take timeouts or breaks, then you won't be able to continue your work for long and it is going to completely burn you out. Slight pressure can make you, but too much pressure can literally break you!

Focusing on the Purpose Rather than Perfectionism

While doing something, perfectionists put all their focus and attention into making sure all the things are flawless, and they tend to forget why they started doing something in the first place! This is very dangerous because nothing is bigger than the purpose. Serving the purpose is the main goal, and it doesn't matter if one or two things don't go as planned as long as it is serving the purpose. If you become paranoid about making things flawless and going as planned, you might end up sabotaging your own journey towards your goal. So, always keep your eyes on the primary purpose and keep reminding yourself why you started doing what you do and why it is important to you. This is the only way you will be able to overlook a few "imperfections" in your plan as long as they are serving the main purpose.

Trying Not to Procrastinate

This is something that most people do. Procrastination is your biggest enemy as it stops you from working. People tend to put off things for the last minute and then end up failing to do it on time or when needed. Planning is obviously important, and so is implementation! If you just keep on planning and thinking about the things you will do but don't actually do them, then you are going to achieve nothing. If you have thought of doing something, just get to work! Don't sit back and keep thinking and planning and re-planning because all of that is a waste of time, and time is very precious as it waits for no one. Don't waste time making unnecessary changes in your plan just because you are still contemplating when to start the actual work! There is only one solution, and that is to stop thinking and get to work!

Getting Rid of the Negative Influences

There will be plenty of negative influences in your life, especially when you are working towards something big and beautiful. A lot of people will try to bring you down! Not just people, but social media, television, podcasts, etc., promote "hustle culture" and "perfectionism"! So, always check what you are consuming from social media and others and what impact it has on you. The moment you see that something is harmful to you, cut it out of your life. Get rid of people who drain you because they do it purposely just so that you don't succeed. You don't have to explain anything to anyone! You don't owe anything to anyone. As long as you know that you aren't doing anything bad, cutting negative influences out of your life is fine. Constructive criticism is good, but unnecessary criticisms and unnecessary opinions are not okay!

Surrounding Yourself With Positivity

As much as getting rid of negative influences from your life, it is important to surround yourself with positivity as well. If you hang out with people who have no ambition, no goals to achieve, and nowhere to reach in life, then someday you are going to end up like them. Only surround yourself with self-driven, ambitious people. This is how you will stay constantly motivated to do good things and achieve great things. Also, it is very important to have people who will support the work you are doing. Don't go around telling every person about your work because you never know who might react in a negative way, which could drain your energy. Instead, share your work-related things with only those people who you think will always support you no matter what. These people are rare, and it is your duty to identify them. Share things with them, and a few positive words from their mouth will do all the magic! Sometimes a few good words can amplify your motivation, which is exactly what is needed to remain focused on your path!

Consciously Lowering the Bar

It is crucial that you recognize that getting things done takes time and that it is a slow process. It can't happen overnight, and it is totally fine to do things at your own pace. You are not a machine, so stop trying to be one. Also, don't compare other people's journeys with yours. Everyone has their separate journeys, and there are a lot of factors and variables that determine the pace and the flow of the journey. So, comparing yours with someone else's is probably the dumbest thing to do, as you will end up worrying for nothing! Also, having too many expectations from yourself is wrong, as you will end up disappointing yourself. So, don't set the bar so high that it gets too difficult for you to achieve!

Keeping the Tasks Bite-Sized

It is very important to break your entire work into small chunks. If you plan to do everything at once, chances are you might fail in your attempt. It is crucial that you keep your tasks bite-sized. It will not only make them more manageable but will also make them easier to do. One of the biggest advantages of this is that once you complete each small task, you will feel a sense of achievement that will boost your motivation furthermore. Small achievements build the momentum, which is very important for sticking to the process in the long run!

Tracking Your Time

It is essential that you keep track of your time. If you don't manage your time effectively, you might find yourself neglecting a lot of important things. Underestimating the time it will take to complete a task, is something you must avoid. Otherwise, you risk not leaving enough time for relaxing and caring for yourself. It is very important to balance your priorities. And that is why you should include some self-care and social activities in your daily schedule. Working and making sure to take part in all other activities takes a lot of self-compassion, patience, and practice. If you follow this over time, you will be able to understand how much time is actually required to do a particular task and how you can incorporate other things into your daily life and still not hamper your work. It will also help you to build confidence that you will be able to complete your work within due time.

Learning the Art of Saying No

Learning to say "no" is something that will help you throughout your life. It is a life lesson that everyone should master. If you struggle to say "no," then people will take advantage of you, and they will make you do things for their own good, knowing that you won't be able to deny them. This will drain you, and you might even end up self-sabotaging your own work. You are the one in charge of your own life, and you have all the right to say "no" to anything. Justifying that is also not mandatory. If you just want to say "no" without giving an explanation, even that is fine! Your mental peace should be your first priority, and that is not being 'selfish"; rather, it is 'kind" to yourself! It is not always a good idea to give it your all, to do what others tell you to do, because not everyone has genuine intentions! Good and kind-hearted people struggle to say "no," and that is what everyone takes advantage of. So, make sure to say 'no" next time someone tells you to do something you don't want to do!

Using the Reward System

Nobody is too old to give small rewards to themselves. Actually, it is one of the best ways to show appreciation and kindness to yourself. Set up small rewards for yourself after completing every small task! It will not only make you happy but will also give you a sense of satisfaction. It will also help in boosting motivation for the upcoming tasks. You will look forward to the next task and will be filled with positivity once you start incorporating this in real-time!

Incorporating Mindfulness

It is extremely crucial to stay in tune with your mindset and body while you are working towards breaking patterns. It is very important to give yourself reminders and breaks in order to avoid feeling overwhelmed. Keep yourself grounded, and it will help you to keep your anxiety under control. When you feel your anxiety kicking in, just take a breather! Go for a walk, or just relax for a while!

Going to Therapy

Lastly, even after trying hard, if you find yourself struggling with wrapping your head around the fact that not everything needs to be perfect, then you can consider seeking professional help as well. Maybe the problem is deep-rooted and just self-determination might not be enough to overcome it! So, it is completely acceptable to consult a therapist to find out what exactly is the cause behind it and how you can deal with it. A lot of people get scared by the idea of consulting a therapist, but you need to understand that it is completely normal to seek a therapist's help. Let them do the tough work for you and help yourself heal with their help!

Chapter 9: Learn to Make Connections and Reach Out

Depression, stress, and anxiety –are quite common, especially in today's world. The world has become a fast-paced and cruel place to live in, and that is exactly why these things have become more common among people nowadays. During these tough times, staying alone and secluded is possibly the worst thing you can do, as it is going to make it even worse!

Depression and loneliness are interrelated to each other in a way. People who are lonely and don't have many connections tend to feel depressed more often. When you feel separated and alone, your depression worsens, and it can have serious consequences. People who feel secluded and isolated are more likely to get the thoughts of suicide or self-harm as they feel nobody cares about them! If a person is a part of a network or community, the chances of him/her getting suicidal thoughts is less! When you have a good community of people around you, you understand that your life is actually valuable and that people actually care about you.

A lot of people think that connecting to others via social media is enough, but it is not! The truth is the more you spend time on social media, the lonelier you tend to feel! Face-to-face communication is very important for you to feel heard and valued! Although the internet has replaced a lot of things, human connection is something that we all need on a regular basis.

Reaching out to people can be difficult, especially when you are depressed. But if you take small steps, it can get easier with time! You can try joining support groups or therapy, where you can freely discuss the things you are going through. These kinds of groups are very helpful, as you will meet people who are dealing with similar issues. So, sharing things with them can be really easy and comforting as well, because you will realize that you are not alone and are going through tough times! This feeling will comfort you and will ease your pain to a great extent. It will also help you build great connections with people with similar mindsets.

Here are a few ways you can try in order to connect and reach out to people.

Family and Friends

It is very important to make new connections, but it is equally important to nourish our connection with our existing friends and family. People often tend to ignore it because they take it for granted. People should be grateful for having a family and the friends that are present in their lives. If you are struggling with stress, anxiety, or depression, connecting to your family might be a great solution. It is definitely going to make you feel safe and comfortable. You can try discussing your problems with them, as they are never going to judge you. Family is the only place where you will get unconditional love, so make sure to receive it and use it to heal your issues! You can even try discussing your problems with old friends and see if they can help you with some good suggestions. Avoiding family gatherings or friend meet-ups is something most people suffering from depression tend to do. You do it thinking that you will stay at home in your own comfort zone, but it actually worsens your mental health!

Making a List of Your Social Connections

Now that you know that you need to connect with people and reach out, you can't just randomly go to anybody and start talking about your issues! You never know how the other person will react or handle the situation. So, it is always a good idea to start by making a list of all your social connections, including your co-workers, social media friends, other friends, and family members. After you have listed down the names, try to identify the ones who are emotionally available, emotionally skilled, as well as emotionally intelligent. These are the ones you would want to go to at times of crisis because they are the ones who know how to handle the situation or what exactly to say to you in order to make you feel better. Empathetic people are rare, but they do exist, and they do exist in your life as well. Just identify them and invite them over for a coffee and start sharing!

Joining an Online Chat Forum

There are times when you are extremely emotionally vulnerable, and you want to talk to someone immediately. These are the times when you can't wait for your friends to come over or get on a call. This is when you can consider joining an online chat forum specially tailored to your requirements. You will meet a lot of people there who will understand exactly what you are going through, and the best part is that you can share all the details of your current situation anonymously, without having to reveal your identity. That is why it is something opted for by a lot of people, especially the ones suffering from social anxiety, as they don't have to go out of their comfort zone. They can just sit at their place and relax!

Participating in a Support Group

Joining a support group can be a great idea in case you feel that you are the only one who is suffering! The support group can be the type where everyone meets in person, or it can even be an online one. The main goal is to bring people together who are having similar issues. Our brains work in fascinating ways. No matter how bad the situation is or how painful something is, you feel an instant sense of relief when you see someone else is going through the same situation. That is exactly why support groups are built. The main intention behind joining a support group is to feel less lonely and to talk to people who are going through the same issues as you. It will not only make you feel lighter but can also be a source of some great suggestions and advice!

Working With a Therapist

Consulting a therapist is not such a bad idea. Some people might believe it is a waste of time and resources and offers little benefit, but they are completely wrong. Taking therapy is a form of self-care that one must do if he/she feels like it! Reaching out for help is not such a bad thing, and what can be a better choice than a professional? Sharing your issues with a therapist will help you release a lot of burden from your mind. The therapists are extremely empathetic individuals who will listen to all your problems and will give you incredible solutions and remedies that will definitely help you feel way better! So never shy out from consulting a professional, and most importantly, never think about what other people will think. Reaching out for help is never a bad thing!

Participating in Group Activities

An incredible way to make new connections and meet new people is through joining group activities. It can be as simple as joining a dance class or taking cooking lessons, etc. These are fun places that can give birth to some amazing and long-lasting connections. These are the places where you meet people with similar passions and interests, so starting a conversation isn't too hard as you already have a common passion for talking. Making new friends can significantly improve your mood because you feel very sociable and confident after doing so. Also, doing the things that you enjoy will keep you occupied and happy. On top of that, if you are doing that with a group of people who enjoy it as much as you do, it is bliss! This will keep you distracted and won't let you feel lonely or depressed.

Visiting a Place of Worship

Synagogues, mosques, and churches are amazing places to go to during emotionally vulnerable times. These are wonderful places to meet new people. People attending religious services tend to have a lot of connections with people. Most importantly, visiting religious places will give you a sense of peace that might heal a lot of your suffering. No matter if you are a religious person or not, religious places are very peaceful in general! There is not much noise or any other distractions. You can simply sit and relax! You can even talk to the religious leaders who will be more than happy to talk to you at times of crisis or need. Make it a habit of attending religious services on a regular basis because that will help you feel less lonely and will also increase the chances of meeting new people and making new connections.

Reaching Out

Reaching out to people or talking out your problems with people is a habit that you have to get used to for your own benefit. It takes time, especially when you have shut yourself down from people for a long time. But make it a point that you need to attend friend meet-ups, and you need to attend family gatherings, social meets, etc. The more you see people, the less your pain will get. Human interaction is very important! If you just sit at home behind your laptop screen, it won't help you very much. You need to see other people in order to remain sane and feel good! Oftentimes, it is seen that others are ready to help you, but you are the one blocking their help, or you are the one pushing them away. It is not only harmful to you but is also harmful to them as well because all they want is to provide you with the help you need!

Addressing Conflict

As much as it is important to make new connections, it is equally important to mend the existing relationships. If you are facing some conflicts or tension within an existing connection, don't keep open ends. Address the conflicts and try to resolve them. Make sure to listen more to the other person and understand their point of view. People often sabotage their existing connections because they don't hear out what the other party has to say, as they are so occupied with their own problems. You have your own problems and stress, but that doesn't mean you should not care about anyone else anymore! If you keep doing that, then you will end up being alone. No matter how much a person cares for you, nobody can tolerate your arrogance or indifferent behavior forever! So, try to hear out their problems as well and mend your current relationships with people.

Cultivating Friendships

Making connections is not all! You need to cultivate friendships as well. Set reminders or make a schedule for reaching out to a person you know that you haven't talked with in a while. Strike a good conversation and get to know how they are doing. This will not only make them feel good but will also make them understand that they have a position in your life and that they matter to you! Try to open up about your problems and the things you are dealing with. You may feel scared to be vulnerable in front of someone else, but have faith that it will make you feel good! Good friends will always be there to listen to your problems and will definitely show up when you need anything. Never shy away from letting people know that they matter to you and that you need help!

Helping Someone Else

Sometimes helping others can be a great way of relieving your own pain. Depression and anxiety might make you feel worthless and unwanted. Once you put some effort into healing someone else or helping someone else out with some of their problems, it will give you an immense sense of satisfaction. You will instantly feel extremely optimistic and good about yourself. When you walk on the road alone, you might feel scared, but then when you walk with a child on that same exact road, you don't feel scared because at that time, you feel protective and responsible for that child's safety, so automatically your will power doubles itself. This is exactly what it is all about. Once you heal someone else, it stimulates a positive cycle, and it also helps you in making really good connections. So, even if a person doesn't ask for it, help them out without expecting anything in return from them!

Avoiding the Mistakes that Come in the Way of Getting to Know People

When you are making new connections, at first, they are strangers to you! Then they slowly become acquaintances, then friends, and finally close connections! The phase where the person slowly becomes an acquaintance from being a stranger is filled with uncomfortable settings, icebreakers, and awkwardness. The mistakes that you need to avoid while making new connections are -

- Firstly, you need to stop continuously talking about yourself. People tend to overdue themselves just to make the other person understand that they are interesting and likable. But that is not how it works. If you go on talking about yourself, you might come off as a person who is full of themself, and that is not the kind of impression you want to create! Also, if you go on talking about yourself, you won't be able to learn much about your new connection.

- Secondly, do not stick to surface-level conversations. People often stick to small talk just to avoid long conversations. This is never going to make the connection deep! If you don't converse about deep meaningful things, your bond will never strengthen! Don't just stick to "Hi, how are you"! Try engaging in deep conversations and discussing meaningful topics, and see how they think! When you talk about the real things, you get to know each other's personality and nature! It is very important to know each other at a deeper level to form meaningful connections!

Maintaining Your Relationships With People

Maintaining your relationships is equally as important as making good first impressions! Do not ignore your current connections, and make sure to say "Hi" once in a while. Making a strong first impression is definitely important, but then if you ignore the person, then all of it will be useless! After making a good first impression, it is observed that a lot of people get too pessimistic, nervous, disorganized, and busy! This is the reason why a lot of good connections end before starting. Do send them a "Hi" once in a while. Do give them a call and talk to them. This will help you maintain a solid relationship with them and will also help them understand that they are important in your life!

Taking 10 Minutes Every Day Just for Casual Talks

One of the possibly worst mistakes that you can make is reaching out to people only during times of need. When you need someone, you should definitely reach out to them and ask for help. But that doesn't mean that you will only remember them when you need help! If someone comes to you only when they need something from you, won't you feel that they are selfish or they are using you? These people will think the same if you do it with them on a regular basis. Take 10 minutes every day from your daily schedule just to have normal conversations with them. Ask them about their day and how they are doing and have a normal conversation. This will make them feel that they are not just present in your life to help you, but they actually mean something to you as well. Next time you are in a crisis, they will be more than happy to help you out and will do everything in their power to make you feel good about yourself!

Getting Rid of the Fear of Rejection

Fear is our greatest enemy. A lot of good connections end before starting out from this fear of rejection. You tend to wonder, what if the other person is not interested in forming a connection, or what if the other person says 'no" when you ask for help. This is something you need to get rid of immediately! You never know how the other person will handle the situation unless you see it yourself. If you shy away from asking for help because of your fear, you will never know what you might be missing out on! Just let go of your fears for once and see what they say or how they behave. They might end up being incredible advisors. You might end up being great friends with them or making deep connections as well! Make sure to get rid of your fears and reach out to them!

Contacting a Hotline

Lastly, if you are feeling extremely emotionally vulnerable or extremely anxious or stressed, you can even try contacting a helpline! There are times when you will feel like totally giving up or harming yourself because of severe depression and anxiety! Staying alone during these times is the worst idea! Also, you might not feel like talking to any friends or family during these times, as you might not want them to see you like that. Hotlines are designed expressly for these kinds of circumstances, and their operators have received specialized training to help you. They know exactly what to say and what to do in that particular situation to calm you down and bring you back to your senses. So, keep a hotline number handy in case you tend to feel like this often! Once you have an episode, make sure that the first thing you do before making any decision is to contact that hotline!

Chapter 10: Art of Letting Go

Depression, anxiety, and stress can be causes of hindrances in the path towards your well-being. They could potentially be caused due to a variety of reasons. Some sudden shock, any unexpected loss or betrayal, some past trauma that is too hard to cope with... the reasons could be many and are subjective. However, one of the main issues that crop up here is the difficulty in letting go of these dark memories. Therefore, the art of letting go becomes one of the most potent tools for you to overcome depression, anxiety, and stress. If you can condition your mind in such a way that even though there are traumatic incidents, you can muster up the strength to let them go, it will become easier for you to not let depression, stress, or anxiety become hurdles in your way.

In this chapter, we will focus on various ways to deal with depression, anxiety and stress, which will help you to let them go and thus, make your life far less demanding and a lot more comfortable. But before we can get to that, let us get a few basics clear. Now that we are talking about the art of letting go, let me ask you about the need for it.

Why Let Go?

You might ask yourself this fundamental question "Why let go at all?" And I will not blame you for that. You see, often times, the present situation might be bad. Say you are no longer in touch with a friend with whom you used to be very close. The reason for the present rift could be many, which lead you to cut off contact with them. But that being said, you have beautiful memories with them from all those good years of friendship. Now you ask yourself, should you also let go of those memories if they were good? The answer is 'yes.' Please understand that letting go doesn't mean you are disregarding those memories. It just means that you have decided not to take them forward anymore. Why? Because when something causes you pain, you should not make more room for it.

What to Let Go of?

The answer to this is subjective. It could be a job, could be a person, could also be a thing. It depends on what is causing you pain and at what stage of life you are in at that moment. If you are a student and one of your compulsory subjects is causing you stress, practically speaking, you cannot do away with it, right? Then, you will need to talk to your teacher and parents and find out doable tricks which will help you get it done. What I mean is, when you find out your reason for your depression, anxiety, or stress, you will have to ask yourself how integral a part of your life that reason is. In most cases, it is, unfortunately, an integral part. So you must find effective ways to let that go, while also not disrupting the fabric of your life.

How Do You Let Go of Something?

We finally come to the question to which everyone is looking for an answer. Once again, how you will let go of something depends completely on you. Different people use different ways to cope with their problems. But more than someone using external methods, the first and foremost requirement is for you to feel the need and have the courage to let go. Once you get that, the rest, though time-consuming, will not be difficult.

In this chapter, we will now look at various ways to deal with and overcome depression, anxiety, and stress. Ways that will help you get the answer of how you can let go of these things individually and collectively.

Ways of Letting Go By Overcoming Depression

Below I will be suggesting a few ways in which you can deal with depression without medicines. Let us find out what they are -

- **Some coping mechanisms for you to try** – Depression comes to different people differently. For some, it might be sitting idle and being unable to move for days on end. For some, it could be doing all the daily chores but feeling hollow from within. For some, it might also be constantly looking for ways of self-harm, etc. But somewhere, all of these are linked with a feeling of detachment from others, and in some cases, with oneself. So, one thing you can try is to keep yourself engaged in a way that will be of service to other people. You need to know that you do make a difference with your presence.

  Another thing you should try is to aim for achievable goals. It is not that you are failing, but probably what you want to achieve is not physically possible at this moment. When you look towards things that are actually doable, you achieve them. And you realize that you were too hard on yourself.

- **Meet whoever you have become** – Who you are today is because of everything you have been through, both good and bad. While it is true that all of us want to forget the bad and remember only the good, it is also not possible to live a life where you dislike one part of yourself just because it is not so good. You have to meet yourself, where you are at that point in your life. The faster you accept yourself, the easier it will be to acknowledge your problems and move on. You will only be able to let go of something when you accept it for what it is. It is justified for you to let go of something bad that you have. But for that, accept yourself fully. It will become easier to look yourself in the eye and move ahead.
- **Your today does not define your tomorrow** – You probably have heard this before, and I will tell this to you once again. Simply because of how immensely true this is. Yes, your past might be painful and bad. You might have done something or gone through something which you are not proud of. But you are only a human being, and you are allowed human mistakes. Stop being so hard on yourself. When you let your past decide your future, you love yourself a little less. When you stifle all your prospects because of something that has happened before, you do not allow others to know the truth, causing them to love you less. You need to know that you are a treasure house of talent and warmth. Do not deprive yourself and the world of that amazing

person by keeping yourself locked in the prison-house of your over-critical mind.

- **Look at the parts and not the whole** – When depressed, what you can try is not to look at the whole but the parts. I hope you realize this, that each and every one of us accomplishes things by conquering the individual parts only for them to add up to become the whole. If you want to climb Everest, you cannot expect to do that one day suddenly without having any prior practice, right? You have to take proper training day after day. Every day that you successfully complete training is a step forward. So instead of fretting about not climbing Everest on the first day itself, look at how many days of practice you have done. That matters more.

These are some of the ways of dealing with depression that you should definitely try. These will help you to let go of all those memories and incidents which are causing depression in the first place. Now, let us have a look at some of the ways you can employ to overcome stress.

Ways of Letting Go By Overcoming Stress

Let us look at some of the easiest ways you can help keep your stress under control and overcome it eventually.

- **Get some physical activity** – Stress has a tendency to bottle up inside you and render you helpless in times of action. This is the very thing you need to contest. You need to indulge in physical activities and exercises to not let stress get the better of you. When you stay immobile under stress, not only does your body stop functioning properly, your mind too becomes prone to overthinking and hyperventilating. With proper action, you will remind yourself what you are capable of, and the stress will remain under control. Have you experienced situations when you are unable to do a certain job because of stress and it causes you more stress? The moment you get up and do it, regardless of the outcome, you are able to get over that stress.

- **Be kind to yourself** – Unless you stop being hard on yourself, negative emotions like stress will never go away. I know it is easier to blame yourself for something that has gone wrong. It comes naturally to us to beat ourselves up for something instead of confronting the other person. Even if the fault was indeed yours, it is damaging to put yourself at gunpoint all the time. Your stress can increase when you do not practice self-care. You taking care of yourself does not have to match with what others do. As long as it is making you happy, it doesn't have to make sense to others. Some find intellectual involvements like reading or writing to be stress busters. If something else works for you, so be it. You just need to make yourself feel alive. You need to be kind to yourself because if not you, then who? Eating, keeping hydrated, and doing things that you love, are things you need to do, not because you have anything to prove to others. But because you owe it to yourself.

- **Speak for yourself** – I need you to understand this, that unless you speak for yourself, no one else will. It is your life, and you have to make sure no one, not even you, should take it for granted. Let us assume that your boss is asking you to stay late because your office is understaffed at the moment. You stay far away from your office, and returning late is not safe. Plus, all this undue extra work is making you tired. All of this adds to your stress and tension. Now, if you wait for someone else to come and save you, that will not happen. Gone are the days when you could rely on others. It is you who needs to muster the courage and go talk with your boss. Either they provide you with extra pay and a place of accommodation, or you do not comply with their undue wishes. It is that simple. The moment you start speaking for yourself, you will learn to assert what is rightfully yours. That way, no one will be able to take advantage of you.
- **Journaling** – Keeping a journal is very useful when you want to deal with stress. Stress, a lot of times, comes from unresolved emotions. Things that you do not, rather cannot share with others, will eventually bottle up inside you, making you stressed and worried. Unless you let go of these emotions, it will be difficult to move ahead or think straight. That is the reason journaling will help you so much. It will be a world of you, for you, and made by you. You can pen down anything without having to worry about others seeing it. You can let go of all your deepest and darkest troubles and secrets. You can write about your emotions,

feelings, wishes, and desires. As long as you do not keep everything trapped inside you, your mind will be free, and your heart will be light. That way, you will be able to deal with the weight of stress in a much more composed manner.

Next, we will talk about anxiety. Just like depression and stress, anxiety has the power to derail you from your intended path. That extreme sense of irritation and discomfort inside you, which is not letting you think straight, but you also cannot seem to let it go. When you are anxious, you might end up doing many things that you wouldn't have otherwise done. At the same time, you might not grasp many opportunities which you would have otherwise taken had it not been for your anxiety. That is why it is crucial to deal with anxiety when you want to master the art of letting go.

Ways of Letting Go By Overcoming Anxiety

- **Talk it out** – The more you let it out, the easier it will be to deal with it. You have to talk it out. It could be a friend, a family member, or a colleague. Basically, anyone whom you are comfortable with and is your confidant. Many times, you get anxious about something because you keep it within yourself. When you share it with others, a lot of times, a solution might come out, or you might get an easy explanation of something. For that to happen, you need to talk it out. Another thing, the more you say something out loud, the easier it becomes to come to terms with. Your voice can do wonders. When you hear yourself say something, your mind and your entire system become accustomed to hearing it. That way, it becomes easier to let go of something. With acceptance comes the power of letting go.

- **It is okay to say no** – If you are not okay with something, you do not owe it to anyone to do it, despite being uncomfortable. It might be something that your best friend has asked you to do, but you are not comfortable with it. But because your best friend has asked you, you are finding it really difficult to say no, which is making you uncomfortable. While I understand your need to say yes to your friend, you have to realize that you, are your own best friend. If you do not support yourself and stand for yourself, it is not possible for others to do so. Your friend will understand if you say a 'no.' Do not push yourself to do anything that makes you anxious. Ask yourself why you are getting anxious or uncomfortable. If you can locate the reason, you can work on it. But even if you do not locate the reason, it is alright to skip it.
- **Take a moment to breathe** – You have to slow down at times and take a good look at everything around you. You can get anxious because a lot is happening, and you do not know how to handle everything. You have an exam coming up, you have two assignments to submit, you have a family function coming up that you cannot ignore, you have a date with your crush, or your best friend is going through some problems and needs your help to solve it... and guess what? What if you have to deal with everything at the same time? What

happens as a result? You get anxious and cannot put your mind to anything. You feel as if you are stranded, and you don't know what to do. What you need to do is take a moment, take a deep breath, and look at all of this individually. When you take these up separately and deal with them, things get in line.

- **Accept that not everything will be in your control** – In the last point, I told you how you should look at tasks individually to handle them better. While that is true, it is also true that there will be some things perpetually out of your control. And it is okay to let them go. When you cannot do them successfully, it does not mean you are defeated. It just means you are a human being, and not everything will be under your control. It does not mean you are losing. It just means that in this universe, there are certain things out of our reach. The faster you accept it, the better it will be for you. When you want to let go of something, accepting your limitations is a big part of it. What you can do instead is focus on things that are under your control. When you look at things that you can do instead of those you can't, you realize you were looking at things from a perspective that was not right for you. When you are a cactus, you need a desert to survive. A rainforest, though beautiful, is not the right place for you. No matter how much you try, a rainforest will not help you survive. A desert, even though it might seem harsh to some, is the perfect place for you to thrive. You just need to understand what is right for you and what is under your control.

All the tips that have been mentioned are ways through which you can let go. Depression, stress, and anxiety are the main reasons behind you being unable to let go of something painful. That is why these useful tips have been mentioned, which will help you deal with these situations individually while enabling you to let go of things that are not right for you. As long as you live in the present, you realize that not the past, not the future, but the present is all that matters. With that understanding comes the realization that expanding your mind's horizon will help you tap into your inner core of strength and power. I hope everything that is not right for you might make its way out of your life.

Conclusion

I hope that you enjoyed reading this book and that it provided you with all the tools necessary to accomplish your goals, whatever those may be. By this point, you should have a solid understanding of the benefits of self-compassion and how to apply it to your own life. You are also skilled in the art of setting and upholding boundaries, as well as the practices of emotional hygiene. You now understand the value of reaching out and you are equipped with the AWARE method for treating anxiety. It was also discussed, how we can treat our depression and anxiety using mindfulness techniques. Finally, we learned about the health advantages of meditation for both your mind and body, and how effective it can be to cope with stress, anxiety, and depression.

By now, you probably have identified some of the factors in your life that are causing depression, stress, or anxiety – whichever of these you are facing. Acknowledging is always the first step and if you have done that – give yourself a pat on the back because it takes a lot of courage. If you are experiencing low moments in your life, don't ever think that you are alone. Instead, find comfort knowing that many people around you are going through exactly the same thing. Most of the time, people don't even see when they fall into the clutches of depression or anxiety, for that matter, and by the time they realize it, they are too deep inside. But like they say – it's never too late to start. So, even if you have just realized it now, start by following the simple steps and strategies you have learned in this book, and you will definitely start noticing the changes in your life!

www.ingramcontent.com/pod-product-compliance
Lightning Source LLC
LaVergne TN
LVHW091056150826
845673LV00002B/593

* 9 7 9 8 8 4 8 2 3 5 2 6 5 *